John A. Brown's, Kerr's & Halliburton's

John A. Brown's, Kerr's & Halliburton's

Where Oklahoma City Loved to Shop

AJAX DELVECKI & LARRY JOHNSON

Published by The History Press
Charleston, SC
www.historypress.net

Front cover: John A. Brown Co., Downtown, 1971. *Photograph by Dave Heaton; courtesy of Oklahoma Historical Society, the Gateway to Oklahoma History.*
Back cover, left: Kerr's Downtown at night, 1960s. *Courtesy of the family of Edward Eason*; *center*: Kerr's Downtown window display, early 1960s. *Courtesy of the family of Edward Eason*; *right*: Postcard of Main Street, 1945. *Courtesy of RetroMetroOKC.*
Opposite: From the 1950s John A. Brown Employee Handbook. *Ajax Delvecki's Collection.*

First published 2016

Manufactured in the United States

ISBN 978.1.62619.360.4

Library of Congress Control Number: 2016937192

Notice: The information in this book is true and complete to the best of our knowledge. It is offered without guarantee on the part of the authors or The History Press. The authors and The History Press disclaim all liability in connection with the use of this book.

To Donna Douglas, 1925–2014
Employee of Kerr's and Halliburton's. Although she never worked at Brown's, she could certainly appreciate that store's quiet philanthropy and Della's admirable business acumen.

Contents

Introduction: "Welcome, Carnivalgoers, to Oklahoma City!" 9

Part I: John A. Brown Co.

1. "You'll Always Have Brown's" 21
2. "As Cheery as a Bright Spring Morning" 26
3. "It's Your Store" 31
4. "Oklahoma City's Most Useful Citizen" 36
5. "Sincerely, D.D. Brown" 42
6. "Welcome to Brown's!" 46
7. "Record Days" 55
8. "Oklahoma Born, Oklahoma Owned, Oklahoma Managed" 67
9. "The Trend!" 76

Part II: Kerr's

10. "There Can Be No Dissatisfaction Here!" 97
11. "The Whole Town's Talking" 104
12. "The Miracle Centers" 116

Part III: Halliburton's

13. "Oklahoma's Wonder Store" 129
14. "The Store with the Friendly Spirit" 137

Epilogue: "Respectfully…" 143
Bibliography 153
Index 155
About the Authors 159

Introduction

"Welcome, Carnivalgoers, to Oklahoma City!"

Oklahoma City was born by presidential proclamation in a single day. On the morning of April 22, 1889, opportunists flooded into the Unassigned Lands for free land and a fresh crack at the pursuit of happiness. By day's end, a tent city of ten thousand settlers had formed a community alongside the Santa Fe rail station.

Some of those settlers who intended on claiming a farmstead arrived in wagons loaded with just enough tools and supplies to establish a claim and probably included no more than a week's rations. However, most of Oklahoma City's pioneers arrived by train from Kansas or Texas, stepping off the passenger platform with a single handbag and limitless hope. For miles and miles, the land on either side of the Santa Fe railroad tracks was devoid of people, farms and crops. Everything the settlers needed—food, lumber, tools—had to be brought in by rail. Still, although the method of founding of Oklahoma City was unique at that time, the process of building a new railroad town from scratch on the open prairie was fairly well developed by 1889, and colonizing retail merchants were part of that process. As it happened, nearly every store in those first few years had originated from a store in Kansas, Texas or points farther east.

Several fortunes were made in those days. The most notable of these was that of William J. Pettee, who later earned the sobriquet "Daddy of Main Street" because of his large, successful hardware store and other Main Street ventures. Pettee, a young twenty-something from northeast Kansas, was dispatched to Oklahoma City from Osage City by his father, who ran a successful store there. On April 23, 1889, Pettee sold a freight car full of building materials and other basic goods directly from the railroad siding in a single day, earning enough capital to seed his hardware store and launch his real estate empire.

Thomas Meriwether Richardson was selected by his family-run lumber company to establish a foothold in the new city. The company had already created a veritable building material empire across Texas and the Southwest, and Richardson arrived a few hours after the land run with a freight car of goods and pre-printed notes with which he could issue credit. Within days, he had converted the merchandise into cash and IOUs and was able to establish not only a permanent store but also what he claimed was the first bank in Oklahoma City.

Generally, though, Oklahoma City slogged through the 1890s. In the first couple years, the city weathered a flu epidemic and a crop failure, which required federal intervention. From the initial 10,000 or so settlers, only about 4,500 remained after the first year. After that, the population leveled out at around 7,000 for most of the decade. Complicating matters, a national depression beginning in 1893 hampered economic growth in the region. That's not to say the boosters were not busy. Led by men like Charles "Gristmill" Jones, Louis F. Kramer and Henry Overholser, the city was able to woo three major railroads and a half dozen smaller ones by the turn of the century. The immediate effect of these railroad-building efforts was that the city was positioned as a regional hub for warehousing and wholesaling goods. No less important was that outside investors observed that Oklahoma City had more going for it than the territorial capital, Guthrie.

Originally, the business district was confined to just a few blocks. Broadway developed along a line parallel to the Santa Fe tracks, and you could find mainly hotels, rooming houses and restaurants along a stretch from California Avenue north to Second Street. Grand Avenue (now Sheridan) was the petty kingdom of Henry Overholser, who owned a majority of the lots along the east–west street. There were few retail stores, and you could find a number of entertainment venues like bars, gambling houses and theaters, including the ornate Overholser Opera House. Main Street was a kaleidoscope of shops and restaurants running west from Broadway to Harvey, most of them twenty-five-by fifty-foot storefronts, packed into the two-block stretch like sardines. Beyond Harvey to the west were mainly homes and rooming houses. First Street (now Park Avenue) was largely industrial because of the presence of the Choctaw and Frisco tracks. Though hard to imagine today, First Street housed grain mills, light manufacturing and plants like the Armour meatpacking facility.

The south and the east sides of the original city were largely undeveloped except for the large warehouse district known as Bricktown today.

At the turn of the century, Guthrie and Oklahoma City were neck and neck in terms of population (about ten thousand each) and influence, but an uptick in the national economy tilted the balance in Oklahoma City's favor. Businessmen—including a budding Anton Classen, soon to be one of the most influential men in the city's history—began an exodus from the capital to its more robust neighbor to the south. Arriving in 1900, Classen began aggressively developing the northwest part of the city, first building on the northern edge and then using the streetcar franchise he owned with John W. Shartel to expand rapidly farther north and west.

That first decade of the twentieth century saw a ferocious boom in the city. Statehood was imminent (1907), and Oklahoma City made no secret of the fact that it was gunning for Guthrie. Boosters made numerous junkets to the east, selling the city at every opportunity and announcing their intent to wrest the state capital from their poorer brethren to the north. It worked. Businessmen continued to flock to town hoping to cash in on this brash, new boomtown. Along Broadway, buildings began to rise above three stories for the first time, and on Main Street, bigger and better stores began offering more variety and greater quality merchandise as middle-class homeowners rode Mr. Classen's streetcar downtown for shopping excursions.

A 1908 postcard of Main Street, looking east from Harvey Street. Kennedy Brothers stands on the right. *RetroMetroOKC.*

The city still strove to put itself into position to win the state capital. Classen and the chamber of commerce, secure in their commercial base, began to promote Oklahoma City as an "industrial prodigy" and were successful in wooing some industry, including the stockyards and two large meatpacking plants; other industries followed. This had the immediate benefit of doubling the population from a 1907 total of thirty-two thousand to sixty-four thousand in 1910 while arch-rival Guthrie was stalled at ten thousand. The twenty-year struggle for the state capital ended that year in an overwhelming victory for Oklahoma City.

Following construction of the state capitol in 1917 and other large civic projects, economic activity in Oklahoma City began to level out. The 1920 census revealed that there were ninety-one thousand people, and for the first time, Oklahoma City had not grown by triple-digit percentages between census years. But another boom was at hand.

Throughout the 1920s, oil fields were discovered all around Oklahoma, though oil had not been discovered in Oklahoma City. Because the city was at the geographic, economic and political center of the state, however, the oil business began to gravitate in Oklahoma City's direction.

The office tower building boom of the early 1920s paid big dividends when oil companies came to town looking for space. The immediate result was the building of even taller towers. The Perrine and Petroleum buildings, built in 1926 and 1927, were the first to truly scrape the sky by passing the ten- and twelve-story heights of their neighbors. This period also witnessed the maturing of the financial services industry in the city as bankers and insurers became adept at handling the special needs of oil producers.

By 1928, wildcatters began test drilling south of Oklahoma City, which was discovered to be at the center of the second-largest pool of oil in the world. In December, the first producing well came in on the south side of the city, and the race was on. Over the next year, derricks began to march north toward the river and the city limits.

The discovery of oil could not have come at a better time for Oklahoma City. Things were so heady in those days that many people didn't seem to notice the stock market crash of 1929. The economic activity associated with the oil industry would help insulate the city from the effects of the Depression for a while.

Emerging from the Depression and World War II, civic leaders like Stanley C. Draper at the chamber of commerce thought an improvement in basic infrastructure would ensure the future growth and economic security of the city. Several highways and expressways were built in, through and

A view of Main Street, 1910s. *Robert Allison Collection, RetroMetroOKC.*

around the city, which helped improve traffic flow but also encouraged suburban migration. To supply adequate fresh water, the city created four dammed lakes and connected them to the city via pipeline. Draper and others also embarked on an expansion campaign, annexing as much land as possible in Oklahoma County and parts of surrounding counties and annexing small towns like Britton in 1950 while making islands of others like the Village.

As with most other cities, GI Bill funding for housing veterans and the subsequent baby boom caused a construction boom, and Oklahoma City sprawled beyond its traditional limits. Expansion was primarily in the northwest quadrant, but growth occurred in all areas of the city. The automobile was the vehicle of choice for these new suburbanites, encouraged by the dismantling of the streetcar system and the new expressways. Retailers had begun to take notice of this as well, and by the middle of the decade, large shopping centers and strip centers with easy front-door parking began to draw business away from downtown.

In addition to the attack on Main Street stores, downtown was beset by an acute lack of parking. Some property owners found it more profitable to raze their buildings and pave them over with surface parking lots, but modern multistory structures were also built to alleviate parking woes. Despite these problems, downtown still grew vertically in the 1950s, and several older buildings expanded or received modern facelifts.

Prosperity finally came to Oklahoma City in the late 1950s, when unemployment and out migration finally leveled off and household incomes tripled. Still, Oklahoma City turned seventy in 1959, and downtown was showing its age, especially in comparison to the shiny new suburbs. Boosters looked forward with great optimism to what they hoped would be the next boom, the Soaring Sixties.

For Oklahoma City, the Soaring Sixties actually began in 1956, when civic leaders first sought federal funds intended for slum clearance and urban development. They set the wheels in motion to refashion the central business district into a first-rate city center capable of competing with Dallas. They turned to noted urban planner and architect I.M. Pei to create the master plan. Approved by the city in 1965, the Pei plan called for the demolition of dozens of buildings in the downtown area, including the Main Street retail district, which it intended to replace with the large indoor Galleria mall. Key

This 1964 urban renewal plan included a monorail zipping through Main Street. *Oklahoma Historical Society, the Gateway to Oklahoma History.*

One of the last stretches of the retail Main Street strip awaits the wrecking ball, 1976. *Photo by Paul B. Sutherland; Oklahoma Historical Society, the Gateway to Oklahoma History.*

features of the new plan were a large convention center, a new dramatic theater and a large botanical garden and lake—all accessible by monorail. In order to make room for these new landmarks, retail merchants and the public were sold on the necessity of ridding the downtown area of blight and older buildings. Using eminent domain and federal funding, the new Urban Renewal Authority would clear those areas, making it possible to build the new structures.

Meanwhile, outside downtown, the city continued to suburbanize in all directions, especially north and northwest. Retail followed the customers as well, making a steady exodus from Main Street throughout the decade. And just as buildings began to fall downtown, developers began eyeing other areas for commercial buildings—soon, new towers and office blocks began appearing along Classen Boulevard and Northwest Expressway.

At the dawn of the 1970s, Stanley Draper promised the new downtown "will be built *for* people—not *away* from people." Gaping holes in the cityscape, their red dirt glare conspicuous from the air, were left behind by several demolitions but later became the sites of projects like the Myriad convention center, large parking structures, Stage Center, E.K. Gaylord Boulevard, Liberty Tower, Fidelity Plaza and the Kerr-McGee headquarters. In 1975, the wrecking ball came for venerable old stores on Main Street like Kerr's and John A. Brown, demolished to make room for the proposed retail Galleria. The spacious indoor Galleria promised to restore downtown shopping to its former glory, but ultimately, it never came to be.

Left: Concerned downtown merchants tried many ways to encourage area shopping, including this Park and Shop promotion from 1970. Oklahoma Historical Society, the Gateway to Oklahoma History.

Below: Though the city ripped out the historical central business district, the planned Galleria project never fully materialized. 1980. *Photo by Al McLaughlin; Oklahoma Historical Society, the Gateway to Oklahoma History.*

The demolitions were a turning point in the public's perception of the urban renewal experience, and a new preservationist sentiment blossomed in the city. By 1977, tens of thousands of people came to see the Biltmore Hotel demolition, though no serious opposition formed to stop it. However, when the previously safe Hales Building was marked for destruction, it set off a wave of protests by preservationists. The building finally fell in 1979. The Oklahoma City retail sector, which began its exodus from the city center in the late 1960s, followed the national trend of consolidation into large malls, namely the mammoth Crossroads Mall in the south and Quail Springs Mall in the far north; Penn Square Shopping Center had plans to enclose its space by the end of the 1970s.

Among other trends continuing in the 1970s was the steady stream of white families moving outside Oklahoma City Public Schools to school districts like Putnam City and Edmond. In 1972, court-ordered busing to integrate the district's schools (the Finger Plan) eventually resulted in a loss of 52 percent of the entire student body and nearly 70 percent of white students. Oklahoma City, known for its boom-and-bust economic cycles, had one final boom caused by the national energy crisis at the end of the decade. The new, lifeless downtown hummed once again, and it seemed the transformation had worked. In the early 1980s, the boom ended in catastrophic bust after the collapse of Penn Square Bank; it would take at least a decade to recover. The end of Oklahoma City's golden age of retail came just months later when John A. Brown department stores were sold to Dillard's.

Part I

JOHN A. BROWN CO.

I

"You'll Always Have Brown's"

The evening of January 7, 1985, was bitterly cold as workers stepped out the door that had been the employee entrance to John A. Brown's Penn Square Mall store since the late 1950s. As a night stock boy for the store, Larry Johnson was frequently the last one out, along with the security officer, who locked the door. On this night, the guard slapped him on the back and said, "Well, when you come back tomorrow you'll be working for Dillard's!" This was the same guy who, months earlier, when Dillard's purchased John A. Brown's and most of the management was relocated, told him, "It pays to be a peon!"

And he was right. *Daily Oklahoman* subscribers in the metro area awoke the next morning to sales ads that simply said "Dillard's" at the bottom where they had said "Dillard's–John A. Brown" the day before. By that time, the name change was just a formality. The date that would go on the tombstone for the legendary Oklahoma City store was September 29, 1984. That was the day the sale of Brown's to Dillard's was finalized following a deal announced on August 9, 1984. There were a few more plots open in the graveyard of Oklahoma City retail, but the dissolution of Brown's really was the death of substantial locally owned department stores.

Poor economic conditions in Oklahoma City caused by the collapse of oil prices in the early 1980s was assumed to be the culprit of Brown's lackluster sales performance. But new owner William Dillard said at the time that his new acquisition was barely profitable because the customer could no longer differentiate between the two stores and Dillard's volume buying power gave it a more robust bottom line.

In retrospect, it seems obvious that the demise of Brown's was always going to be at the hands of Dillard's. Opening his first dry goods store in tiny Nashville, Arkansas, in 1938, William T. Dillard set a course for a retail empire building based on expansion and acquisition. Limiting himself to the Southwest, he identified potential markets for expansion and purposely stayed out of the larger, more mature markets like Dallas–Fort Worth and St. Louis until conditions were to his liking. He realized Oklahoma had no aggressive retail expansionists, nor had it attracted great attention from other expansionists in the Southwest or nationally until Federated Stores bought Halliburton's in 1947.

Despite what one would assume to be humble beginnings in rural southwest Arkansas, William Dillard was no rube. Born into a family of grocers, he had a firm understanding of retailing that he applied to his studies at the University of Arkansas and as a graduate student at Columbia University's business school. At the age of twenty-three, he moved to Nashville, ten miles north of his hometown, and opened T.J. Dillard's Dry Goods with his father's name and $8,000 of his money. He returned $42,000 in sales the first year.

A decade later, he acquired enough cash and experience to purchase family-run stores in Magnolia, Arkansas, and Texarkana and Tyler, Texas. Throughout the 1950s, he continued to focus on identifying struggling stores with poor prospects in small markets around the Southwest. He purchased them at their lowest value and then relied on quickly turning the stores around and back to profitability. Along the way, Dillard proved to be an early adopter of trends, such as the shift to suburban stores and innovations like computerized inventory tracking. The Dillard success formula had three tenets. The first was to offer top-quality national brands that were backed by national advertising campaigns; the second was to offer pleasing prices through volume purchasing; the third was so important that Dillard engraved it on a plaque in his office, "Business without integrity is not good business and in the long run will not be successful."

Dillard kept a close watch on Oklahoma because its two major cities had strong retail players (like Brown's, Kerr's and Halliburton's in Oklahoma City and Brown-Dunkin and Vandever's in Tulsa) and yet, unlike Dillard's and Sanger-Harris, Federated and other chains, those players did not seem bent on expanding or acquiring each other, let alone acquiring stores in other cities or states. To Dillard, that signaled eventual failure.

As it happened, his first foray into Oklahoma happened quite by chance. Dillard had fashioned strong relationships with several vendors of quality merchandise (e.g., Van Heusen shirts) as well as bankers across the Southwest. During a visit to St. Louis in 1959, Dillard was approached by a representative from the First National Bank of St. Louis with an inquiry as to whether he would be interested in purchasing the Brown-Dunkin department store in Tulsa. The store's co-founders, John A. Brown and John H. Dunkin, had died in previous years and the once profitable store had since run up sizeable debts with several banks and merchandise vendors. Impressed with the performance of his stores, the debtors offered to assist Dillard in putting together a deal to buy out the venerable old Tulsa institution. In early 1960, Dillard had completed what was essentially a leveraged buyout, as his $6 million company acquired the assets of a $10 million company. As the *Tulsa World* put it, one of the "giants of the Southwest" had fallen.

Most observers doubted that Dillard could turn around the venerable old Brown-Dunkin. He immediately sold his Texarkana store to finance a complete renovation of his new ten-story store. True to his tenets, he also upgraded the quality of merchandise available and doubled the advertising budget, as well as introduced the daily sales quota. Dillard could calculate to the penny the dollar value of sales each store had to attain every day in order to be profitable. This was true of all Dillard's stores, and all of those who worked for him knew all too well the anxiety of a slow day on the sales floor. If it looked like the store would be short for the day, executives, managers and salespeople slashed prices, built up displays and even took to the phones (including Dillard himself) to let customers know of values available that day at the store. Within eighteen months, Brown-Dunkin was profitable and all debts had been retired.

Bolder from his success in Tulsa, William Dillard continued to expand his department store empire. In 1963, he purchased the two largest chains in Little Rock, Pfeifer's and Gus Blass, both of which had histories dating back to the post–Civil War era. Still, he had only downtown stores in his quiver. He knew that the future of retail was in the suburban shopping malls already appearing in large cities on the coasts. In 1964, he partnered with Sears & Roebuck to develop the Southland Shopping Center, a new indoor mall in Austin, Texas. He also moved his family from Tulsa to Little Rock that year, telling the press, "I'm from Arkansas. I know someone from every town in the state."

He never took his eye off Oklahoma, though. Over the next few years, he added a handful of new suburban stores to his empire, including two new

Brown-Dunkin stores in Tulsa at Northland and Southroads. By 1967, he was finally ready to enter the state's biggest market. In 1964, Kerr's, John A. Brown's biggest competitor, moved into Shepherd Mall, the state's first air-conditioned indoor shopping center at Northwest Twenty-Third and Pennsylvania Streets adjacent to a large freestanding Sears store. It was a case of too little too late for Kerr's, and the company began to flounder. Three years later, Dillard purchased the store and installed his Brown-Dunkin brand as the mall's north anchor. This was the tip of the spear for Dillard's in Oklahoma City. Over the next decade or so, he continued to develop mall stores at Crossroads (1973), Sooner Fashion (1976), Heritage Park (1978) and Quail Springs (1980), often going head to head with John A. Brown's in the same mall.

The Quail Springs store was heralded as Dillard's fifth store in metro Oklahoma City, the eighth in the state and fiftieth overall. Although John A. Brown had been purchased by Dayton-Hudson in 1971 (outbidding Dillard), there had always been a degree of autonomy in how the store was run, and the corporate leadership in Minneapolis had already begun to shift its focus to discount stores Target and Mervyn's. As such, Brown's was never able to capitalize on the buying power of the corporate parent, which left Brown's at a disadvantage with the sprawling Dillard's franchise. The collapse of Oklahoma City's economy only accelerated the demise of Brown's, which saw sales decline steadily each quarter in 1983–84. By contrast, the more efficient Dillard's actually increased its sales in Oklahoma by 10 to 12 percent.

In mid-1984, when Dayton-Hudson decided to unload John A. Brown, it invited Dillard's and its regional rival Sanger-Harris to bid for the six Brown's stores and a twelve-store chain in Arizona and Nevada called Diamond's. Sanger-Harris was very interested in the Arizona property, and it had some interest in entering Oklahoma City; however, it felt that the retail landscape was not favorable to new players there. Dillard's truly lusted after Brown's, but Arizona was not in its expansion plans. When Sanger-Harris opted out, William Dillard knew the offer was too good to pass up. He made an offer on July 7, 1984.

Over the next month, rumors flitted about the city's malls as the fraternity of store managers, buyers and vendors circulated news of the sealed offer. Finally, on August 8, 1984, James Miller, president and CEO of Brown's, sent a letter to employees informing them of the sale (which he blamed on lackluster sales from a sagging economy and intense competition) and encouraging them to maintain the high degree of professionalism he had come to expect from them.

This was the final ad using the John A. Brown name, January 27, 1985. *From the* Daily Oklahoman.

Dillard's phased the transition from Brown's over a period of months. The name immediately became Dillard's–John A. Brown. Corporate officers moved to new postings at Dayton-Hudson while Brown's warehousing and merchandising operations were shifted to the regional office in Fort Worth. In November, the John A. Brown furnishings, signs and other corporate property was auctioned in a public sale; the Brown's store at Campus Corner in Norman, the Crossroads and Quail Springs stores and the Woodland Hills Mall store in Tulsa were closed; and Utica Square in Tulsa and Penn Square in Oklahoma City were converted to Dillard's.

The sale of Brown's meant locally owned traditional department stores in Oklahoma City vanished. In fact, the sale made Dillard's the largest traditional department store chain in the country. William Dillard never revealed the price he paid for John A. Brown, although Dayton-Hudson later confirmed a price of $140 million for the eighteen-store package. Whenever the terms of the deal came up, he would say only that he bought Brown's real estate and its accounts—he didn't pay a penny for the name. And on January 8, 1985, the name John A. Brown ceased to exist.

2

"As Cheery as a Bright Spring Morning"

When William T. Dillard deliberately noted that he paid nothing for the John A. Brown name, the insult was not lost. There was a reason that Brown's was the sole surviving locally owned traditional department store in Oklahoma, and it had everything to do with the man and the name John A. Brown.

Longtime Brown associate Eliot Lyon remembered that the first time he ever met John Albert Brown was at a social event for his literary study club in Emporia, Kansas. Lyon was instantly struck by Brown's intelligence and affable charm. Of course, he already knew the name Bert Brown because practically every woman he met in the bustling railroad town mentioned him when she was complimented on her apparel. He also found it remarkable that Brown, the silks, woolen goods and fabrics salesman at Rorabaugh's Dry Goods Store, knew the names of all his customers and their previous purchases.

In those days, ready-to-wear had not yet caught on, and shoppers constructed outfits by purchasing fabrics, trims, buttons and other items and sending them to a dressmaker or tailor for construction. The fabrics department was the most important department in a dry goods store, and salesmen like Bert Brown could make or break the success of a store. Each customer who came to his counter received personal attention; Brown made enquiries about her personal taste, favorite colors, the occasion for the clothing and other details, all of which he copiously recorded in notebooks. He used the information to notify customers when new merchandise arrived and to better inform the store's buyers when purchasing goods at market. He also cultivated acquaintances with his customers, often greeting them on the street and around town, asking after their families and complimenting them on their completed outfits. The result was a large following, to the extent that customers would come into the store early and sometimes wait hours for the great Bert Brown to dress them. So whether at a dry goods counter in a small town or the electronics department of a big-city mall store, the name John A. Brown came to signify friendly, personal service. It was a name everybody in Oklahoma knew.

John Albert Brown was born in Nimishillen township, a few miles northeast of Canton, Ohio, in 1878. The Brown family worked an average hundred-acre farm like most families in the area, and his father, Dexter, also maintained a stand of timber with a sawmill. In Stark County, Bert grew up among several generations of Browns and his mother's Pennsylvania Dutch family. But it was a family with roots back to the beginning of Ohio that would change the course of his life—the Rorabaughs.

Bert Brown was studious, and Ohio friends recalled that he was frequently seen with his head in a book, taking every opportunity to read on the walk home from school and in between farm chores. Still, he completed the standard eight grades at the county school and accepted his apparent fate to a life of hard labor on the farm at the age of thirteen. However, during the holiday season in 1900, his family received the annual Christmas letter from his aunt Susan Rorabaugh, his father's sister, in Altamont, Missouri, just north of Kansas City. Amid the annual recap of the family's year was a casual invitation for any of the Ohio clan to "come on down" to Altamont for a visit. Burdened with the boredom of farm life, Bert convinced his father to let him take her up on the offer.

Once in Missouri, Bert Brown was found to be quite charming, which caused his aunt to conspire with him to convince his family to let him stay indefinitely. She persuaded her son, Anson Otterbean Rorabaugh, to take on young Bert at his dry goods store in Emporia, Kansas. Rorabaugh, an older cousin, had a dramatic effect on the course of the twenty-one-year-old's life.

Like Brown, A.O. Rorabaugh had been destined for a life on the farm. But when his mother inherited $125, she used the money for an education for her son. He made good on his opportunities. He established himself in business in northern Missouri, where the poor roads and mountainous terrain of the area presented several challenges for store owners. But Rorabaugh took the innovative step of printing up two-color flyers with information about his products and prices and delivered them by horseback all through the countryside. Along the way, he got to know the people on his routes and learned their preferences, just as Bert Brown would do later. He did well enough but eventually opted for better conditions in Topeka and then Emporia, Kansas, with its access to two major railroads. Over the next twenty years, Rorabaugh built somewhat of a retail empire in Kansas, with stores in Emporia, Newton, Hutchinson, Salina and Wichita, Kansas, and Decatur, Illinois.

When Bert Brown first came to the Emporia store, his cousin found he still had the manners of a country boy from Ohio, and he wasn't allowed to wait on customers. He was apprenticed to C.V. Oldfield in the display department, where he learned to trim windows and also managed the stock in the fabrics department. There he quickly learned about the merchandise and how to handle customers, and he was soon on the selling floor wowing his female fans.

By 1905, Brown was unhappy with his position and the money he was making at Rorabaugh's, and he answered an ad for a buyer in women's wear at the H. Herpolsheimer store in Lincoln, Nebraska. During a two-year sojourn at Herpolsheimer, he was buyer for women's wear and later the linens and wash goods (everyday dress fabric that remained colorfast in a washing machine) departments. He also recruited his old friend Eliot Lyon in Emporia to come to Lincoln and work for him.

In 1908, Bert Brown was approached by the Johnson Larimer Dry Goods store in Wichita with an offer to assume control of the Fair Department Store, a bankrupt store they had recently acquired in Guthrie, Oklahoma. Brown did all the buying, and he again brought Lyon with him to help manage the store. Lyon recalled in the early days, "We worked very hard to gain business and re-establish the concern in Guthrie. Night after night we would return to the store to get displays out, sign cards placed and everything ready for the next day's business....[We] tried to get to know as many people in Guthrie and the surrounding country as possible. We both carried notebooks in which we entered the names of people we met and we developed a large acquaintance and following during the years in Guthrie."

After a few months, Brown brought in A.O. Rorabaugh as a partner. Together they bought the store from Johnson Larimer, and it became part of Rorabaugh's chain. In September 1908, they liquidated all the old Fair Store merchandise and reopened as Brown Dry Goods Company. To aid in the success of the business, C.V. Oldfield came over from Emporia to handle the display department, and other Rorabaugh's people came over as department heads as well.

Over the next seven years, Brown and Lyon made the Guthrie store work well enough, but after the state capital moved to Oklahoma City in 1910, Guthrie entered a downward trajectory from which it would never recover. Every ambitious businessman in Guthrie knew it, and a steady stream of companies made the short trek south to Oklahoma City over the next decade. At the same time, A.O. Rorabaugh was consolidating his own retail empire into "the greatest department store syndicate in Kansas." By 1915, he had purchased the controlling interest in the Brock Dry Goods Company in Oklahoma City with an aim to move Brown and the Guthrie store to greener pastures in the capital.

The new store at 213–19 West Main Street was named Rorabaugh-Brown Dry Goods Company. Rorabaugh and Brown intended the Oklahoma City store to be an entirely new operation rather than a relocation of the Guthrie store or a merger with Brock. Although the new store was part of the Rorabaugh group and received all the advantages of expertise and volume purchasing from the group, it was Bert Brown's store. He was responsible for all its operations. After fifteen years learning the trade, John A. Brown finally reached a station truly befitting his talents.

Almost immediately, the store took on the characteristics of its leader. Bert Brown was a notably kind man, known for his empathy for both his employees and his customers. He often attributed a lot of the success of the company to his employees, whom he saw as his family, and worked long hours every day, often alongside them out on the sales floor. For him, his store was more than simply a place for earning money—it was a training ground for life and business. He knew well the hardships he had in life on the farm and in business, and he was eager to relieve those same conditions for his employees. To that end, he was always keen to recognize talent in his employees and encourage them to start businesses of their own. For a time, there were dozens of thriving business owners in Oklahoma who could point to Brown's mentoring as a key to their success. Not least of these was his brother-in-law, John H. Dunkin, whom he installed as a partner in the Brown-Dunkin stores in Tulsa in the 1920s.

The most acute part of any training a person received from John A. Brown's was in the realm of human relationships. Brown told his employees that the company was not about "selling fashionable merchandise—but an institution founded on the interests of people." Asked what his store's personnel policy was, he replied:

> *The employees of the Browns store are hand-picked. Only those having the highest possible degree of intelligence and character are considered, for they are entrusted with the responsibility of taking care of Brown's customers, a function that demands the keenest of comprehension, unfailing courtesy, friendliness and spontaneous desire to serve. These employees are constantly undergoing training for the purpose of increasing their efficiency and developing their talents.*

Or, as he succinctly exhorted his employees, "The customer is an invited, honored guest to the store—welcome him accordingly."

That undying commitment to the customer was so powerful that it continued all the way into the dying days of the company and still does live on in many of us who worked for Brown's as we carry that spirit into our varied careers today. Any question about what the impact might have been on the customer could be answered by storyteller Molly Rogers Lemmon, who incorporates Brown's into her family lore. "Brown's department store covered an entire city block from the basement to the top of the fifth floor. You could buy anything you needed from garden supplies, crystal, china, jewelry, clothes; it didn't matter. John A. Brown's had it all. And we felt like, in our family, that we owned that store."

3

"It's Your Store"

Feeling like they owned the place is exactly what Bert Brown wanted for his customers.

Before leaving Guthrie, Bert met a sophisticated young vocalist and music teacher named Della Mae Dunkin. Strong, sensible and beautiful, Della seemed the perfect complement to the ebullient Bert. She was later described in print as "a most able assistant of her husband in the Guthrie store," but the degree of her involvement is not widely known today.

Eliot Lyon, who had been the only buyer and Bert Brown's right-hand man in the Guthrie store, came with him to Oklahoma City. In addition to bringing Lyon, Bert allowed most of the Brock's employees to stay on with the new store. One of them was Brock's office manager, Laura Ambrose, who had been a teenaged secretary when Brock's first opened and would later become a key player in the future success of John A. Brown's. From the outset, Brown wanted his employees to feel like family not only with him but also with one another.

Laura Ambrose remembered that Bert brought an infectious sense of fun to the staff. Many decades later, she recalled that in the early days, store meetings were held at the foot of the stairs and often times consisted of singing amusing songs. Other times, the staff would resort to good-natured ribbing like the time the store closed for inventory and deep cleaning and the department manager with the dirtiest area found a live pig waiting in his office. Eliot Lyon attributed the fun atmosphere to one word: *enthusiasm*. Bert Brown was so enthusiastic about the store that it carried over to his employees. And it was these same motivated and enthusiastic employees who made the customers feel at home and like they owned the place.

One of the byproducts of the high-spirited Rorabaugh-Brown's workforce was an innovative attitude. Brown encouraged his managers and associates to try new things to bring in new business and reminded them that their greatest asset, their greatest advertisement, was the satisfied customer. Just months after opening, the store cleared out its basement and created the wonder-filled Toyland with rotating special toys (including swords, working cannons and air rifles) and a visit from Santa Claus on the Saturday following Thanksgiving. Department store Santas were not unheard of, but Rorabaugh-Brown's also gave away to children one thousand wooden Santa Claus cutouts that featured a velvet sack filled with candy. Mothers were advised, "We had a local candy shop prepare this candy specially for us and we guarantee it to be absolutely pure—so you need not worry about the children becoming ill from eating it."

Lyon also created the Bargain Square near the main entrance, which allowed managers to experiment with products and prices and provided a sense of mystery to shoppers because they never knew what would be on

An already expanding Rorabaugh-Brown's gets ready for a Main Street Christmas, 1920s. *Oklahoma Historical Society, the Gateway to Oklahoma History.*

the Bargain Square. One day, they even sold a wagonload of cucumbers they bought off a grocery wholesaler who happened to pass the store that morning, even though the store did not carry fresh produce.

Another tactic was to hire experts to teach customers a particular skill (usually involving a particular product at a special price in the store). Experts were all the rage in the Progressive era, and Brown's brought in artists to teach painting or to exhibit master works of art and beauty experts like Dr. Martha Turner, who provided a week's worth of free lectures on how to retain one's good looks. "You will never regret coming to hear Dr. Turner," shoppers were advised. "The one woman who has defied the encroachment of advancing age by the use of face creams and powder. Hear Dr. Turner tell her own story of her extreme beauty at the age of 43."

There were many other gimmicks in those early days, like passing out "lucky" pennies to shoppers, but by far the strangest ploy and the one that loyal Brown's shoppers and employees talked about for years happened during the annual Baby Week sale in April 1925. Baby Week at Brown's had become an institution for Oklahoma City mothers over the previous decade. There were always special prices on wonderful merchandise, baby-raising experts and free baby photo shoots. Shoppers in 1925, however, were at first amused to see the signs announcing that "REAL LIVE BABIES will be here from 10 a.m. to 4 p.m. to welcome all mothers and prospective mothers!" Certainly that had potential for adorableness, but the signs also announced, "OTHERS MAY BE ADOPTED—Yes, they are orphans—you will love them instantly and want one for your very own—and may have one—provided you meet the requirements—see them every day this week—at Rorabaugh-Brown's." Forty years later, Laura Ambrose recalled that the store received so many offers to adopt the orphan babies that store executives had to make Solomon-like decisions on who should have them. Unfortunately, state laws and the lack of corporate records prevent us from knowing which children were adopted and what became of them, but it would be fascinating to know.

Because he was loving, jovial and personable, it would be easy to overlook Bert Brown's business skill. When he convinced Rorabaugh to partner with him, Bert brought only $1,000 cash to the table, but the company succeeded because of his policies and the better conditions in Oklahoma City. He worked closely with his buyers and passed along his uncanny knack for identifying what customers wanted. He instructed them in how to obtain the best possible prices for the goods—all the while reinforcing his belief that they owed the customer, not necessarily the company, their best effort

John A. "Bert" Brown, Oklahoma City's Most Useful Citizen, 1930. *Oklahoma Historical Society, the Gateway to Oklahoma History.*

and service. As a result, the store began to sell in tremendous volume from the outset, even drawing the attention of a national retail magazine that was amazed that the store did over $100,000 in sales each week and did not even own a warehouse because of the speed with which they turned over the merchandise. Brown said the reason was that he had a "buying force" instead of the usual selling force—his buyers were sellers and his sellers were buyers. With the solid financial foundation, the loyalty of his workforce and the adoration of large swathes of Oklahoma consumers, Bert Brown was poised to turn this winning combination into an expansive southwestern retail empire.

4
"Oklahoma City's Most Useful Citizen"

By the mid-1920s, Oklahoma City shoppers were already familiar with the prominent Brown's Main Street storefront, and the store was beloved for its quality merchandise at reasonable prices and service that put the customer first. Through advertising in small-town newspapers and offering to refund the price of a rail ticket into the city with the purchase of Brown's merchandise, the store extended its notoriety around the state.

In 1924, flush with cash, Bert Brown took a page from A.O. Rorabaugh's book and seized an opportunity to buy out Hunt Mercantile, the largest department store in Tulsa. Nearly a decade earlier, when the offer was made for Brock's in Oklahoma City, he had been told that the small volume store would never be able to challenge its two big competitors, Kerr's and Halliburton's. This time he was buying in at the top of the market.

The Hunt Mercantile store was similar to Rorabaugh-Brown in that it had developed into a regional giant in retailing. Under owner Daniel Hunt, the store had a commanding market share in northeastern Oklahoma as well as neighboring parts of Missouri, Arkansas and Kansas, dubbed by boosters as Tulsa's Magic Empire. Just months before the buyout, Hunt completed construction on a $525,000 three-story Art Deco–style building in downtown Tulsa at Fourth and Main Streets. The *Tulsa Tribune* quipped, "Evidently the Hunt Department Store meets with no sales resistance since the owner is spending one half million dollars to erect the large building."

One close observer to Bert Brown's financial wizardry was his brother-in-law, John Haskell Dunkin. He apprenticed himself up the ladder from the store's shipping department to a position as company secretary, just behind Brown and Lyon in rank. Brown established a partnership with his relative and installed him at the top of the new Tulsa enterprise. Bert ponied up $1.25 million for the Hunt buyout and gave Dunkin the same terms he had gotten back in 1908 when the Guthrie store opened. The Hunt store was renamed Brown-Dunkin, with Brown as president and Dunkin as vice-president, but Dunkin was to have a free rein in operating the Tulsa store. As far as can be determined, the new store was not part of the Rorabaugh chain, although there were occasional references in advertising of "our Tulsa store." A profile of A.O. Rorabaugh in a Kansas newspaper listed Tulsa among his covey of stores, so all the stores were certainly in cooperation.

Back in Oklahoma City, Rorabaugh-Brown's began to grow physically just as its market share had grown. In 1925, after the Brown-Dunkin transfer was complete, Brown's added the building at 221–23 West Main Street adjoining the store on the west side, which added three stories and a basement (expanded to the full six stories in 1928). The following year, the first floor and basement of 210–12 West First Street was leased. This location was directly behind the original store building across an alley, and customers could enter through the storefront on First Street or cross the alley from the Main Street building. In 1927, the three-story building on the east side of the original Main Street storefront was added. Customers would no longer have to dodge delivery trucks in the back alley after a covered bridge was built that connected the second and third floors of the original building with the new additions.

During this great expansion in size, Brown's also expanded its services. Going back even to the Brock's days, there was the Oval Room, which was an ornate room decorated with gossamer sheer drapes and featured a small raised platform for models to exhibit clothes and furs for prospective buyers. But in the early 1930s, the store began to offer the services of Marilyn Arbee as personal shopper. Brown's took the personal shopper a step further than other stores by partnering with WKY radio. Using WKY's experimental shortwave broadcasting equipment during the Christmas season of 1933, the station did its first live remotes when it followed Arbee as she strolled through Brown's 106 departments pointing out interesting gift items, new merchandise and bargains for listening shoppers. Her daily broadcasts were so popular that a second program was added, and both programs were continued well into the 1940s. Marilyn was not a real person, of course, but rather a personification of the store's personal shopping department (her last name was a phonetic spelling of the store's initials, R-B).

Brown's also began to vastly expand its reach in this era. They had always offered telephone and mail service and enticed regional customers into the store with extended advertising coverage in small town newspapers. By 1930, the store was doing such tremendous volume that they employed nearly two-dozen vehicles delivering purchases all over central Oklahoma and providing installation for items like draperies, radios and appliances.

Beginning in the late 1920s, they also started offering air service. Partnering with large-scale air carriers like the new Braniff airlines, Brown's became the first store in the region to allow customers to make special orders from around the country and receive them by air freight in just a day or two. Brown's buyers in Europe even shipped special orders via the *Graf Zeppelin* airship after 1932 until the *Hindenburg* disaster effectively ended airship travel in 1937. The cost was ultimately too expensive and available planes and pilots too irregular for the service to continue, but in today's world of global airfreight and drone delivery, it's clear that Brown's was on the leading edge of retail service in this region.

The late 1920s and early 1930s also saw expansion of another sort as Bert's business acumen and charitable heart led to greater roles in the community. In addition to pouring his seemingly boundless energy and creativity into his store, he also made his talents freely available to various charitable organizations by serving in leadership roles. As such, he was selected as the unanimous choice for Oklahoma City's Most Useful Citizen of 1930. The following year, he did a turn as the president of the chamber of commerce. This was little shock to longtime Brown partner Eliot Lyon, who always maintained that Bert Brown "had a superior judgment in operating the store and was most efficient as an organizer. He anticipated moves that should be made to meet economical conditions and was seldom incorrect."

The culmination of Bert's success in the department store business, on a personal level, came in February 1932, when Rorabaugh transferred sole ownership of the store. Bert became president of the new John A. Brown Company and appointed brother-in-law John H. Dunkin as vice-president. The new company included Brown-Dunkin in Tulsa, which would retain its name, but Rorabaugh-Brown would change gradually to John A. Brown's over the course of the next year in the same fashion as the transition from Brock's had been.

During the Great Depression, Bert took every opportunity to relay calm, reassuring messages to his customers and his staff. A particular concern was staff morale. He knew his employees read about mass layoffs in newspapers, saw the breadlines on newsreels or even had unemployed family members and were afraid the same would happen to them. He regularly reassured them that he would do everything in his power to guide the company safely through the tempest. He told them that changes in the store's operation would be made as necessary to bring customers into the store but closing the sale was their responsibility. A common tactic he used was to encourage them to present the value of an item rather than its price. "The John A. Brown Company is not merely an institution selling fashionable merchandise," he told them in 1934, "but an institution founded on the interests of the people. We are continually trying to promote public economy through the medium of dependable merchandise at honest values." To that end, he often shared his "Selling Saws" with staff, reminding them, "Very few people know values—show the customer why quality goods are worth the price"; "Talk about the service your commodity renders—that is what the customer buys"; and "Never argue questions of taste—logic can never make a man like olives." As far as can be determined, the John A. Brown Company never laid off a single employee because of economic conditions.

As a show of faith, he expanded the store yet again by acquiring the last storefront between Brown's and the Hales Building and the three-story

The downtown store held a loyal following up until its very last days. *Kenyon Morgan Collection, RetroMetroOKC.*

building between Brown's and the Alexander Drug Company warehouse on First Street for a total expansion of twenty-six thousand feet. This expansion, he said, would put more people to work and would increase the earning power of every employee at Brown's.

Brown's also remodeled some spaces and experimented with new techniques in order to continue serving their loyal customers who had fallen on hard times. For one, the basement was converted into a bargain center that offered seconds, remnants and close-out merchandise at affordable prices. Brown's also held the area's first White Elephant Sale, offering great values on a wide variety of products, including display items, mismatched shoes, odd colors and sizes or simply an oversupply. The White Elephant Sale quickly grew into a popular Brown's tradition in Oklahoma City.

The one move Bert Brown made that deepened the love and respect Oklahomans had for him was his relaxation of his credit policies. "Liberality is the dominant note," he told his credit department. "Above all, make the things the people need available without burdening them further. There is to be no discrimination between persons but rather, the same consideration for all." In response, the credit department varied the rates and payment terms to make necessities like winter coats and school clothing affordable and extended longer terms for items like household furnishings. This relaxed credit policy was remembered by loyal Brown's customers for many years and was often mentioned during the mourning over the Dillard's buyout.

As 1940 dawned, Brown's began preparing a grand twenty-fifth-anniversary celebration. However, in January, Bert and Della traveled to the Mayo Clinic for Bert's annual medical evaluation. On Thursday, January 25, John Albert Brown died from a heart attack in a Rochester hotel room. Reporting the news back home, the *Daily Oklahoman* said, "It is doubtful any man in Oklahoma City took a more active part in the city's business and civic life than Brown."

Bert's funeral was held the following Monday at the First Methodist Church. Over 1,500 were in attendance, and observers remarked that the building was so crowded with mourners that the coffin, altar and choir were completely hidden from view. Judge Edgar S. Vaught presided over the funeral and remarked, "This good man was my friend. No worthwhile enterprise in Oklahoma City has been without the support of John A. Brown. We should hold his memory before the youth of this community as an inspiration of what an ordinary country boy can accomplish."

As nearly two dozen honorary pallbearers lined the path to the hearse, the coffin was carried by active pallbearers whose roster reads like a history book of Oklahoma City: E.K. Gaylord, G.A. Nichols, Hugh Johnson (First National Bank), Tom Braniff, Frank Buttram, J.H. Everest, W.S. Bulkley (Kerr's), J.C. Halliburton, Robert A. Hefner and Stanley Draper. Bert was laid to rest in the mausoleum in Fairlawn Cemetery.

Della was all alone.

5

"Sincerely, D.D. Brown"

After the throng of mourners slowly dispersed from Fairlawn Cemetery on North Shartel, Della Dunkin Brown entered the familiar, long black car she and Bert took to the store every day. The drive to their sprawling villa in bucolic Nichols Hills on mostly unpaved roads was much longer than it is today, but it must've seemed like an eternity for Della. Over the last ten years at 1601 Guilford Lane, the estate had become her refuge from public life, and with Bert gone, she risked it becoming her prison. She was an introvert, sure, but she never intended to live a life of seclusion. Neither had it ever occurred to her that she would someday have to run Bert's business—his life's work—without him.

Della Mae Dunkin was born into a farming family, but she was raised to be a middle-class woman of refinement, educated in liberal and fine arts, trained in social graces—and the perfect wife for a businessman like Bert Brown. Las Vegas in the New Mexico Territory was, at the time of her birth there in 1883, one of the wildest places in the Wild West. Notable historical figures who lived there around the same time as the Dunkins include Wyatt Earp, Doc Holliday and Billy the Kid, and the vicinity was subject to raids by Apache warrior Geronimo until his capture in 1886.

The Dunkins moved to northwestern Missouri a few years after Della was born, and she and her four brothers grew up outside Kansas City. After completing eight years of school, Della enrolled in Woodland College in Independence, Missouri. She showed great promise in several musical instruments, particularly piano, and after graduating from Woodland, she went to Chicago to attend the Busch Conservatory of Music, specializing in piano and vocals. She completed her musical education by studying in Italy for several months.

In 1905, after finishing her courses at the conservatory, Della moved to Guthrie, where her parents had relocated. She made a sufficient living providing private music lessons to local children and performing in churches and concerts around town. It was in one of these concerts, held at the Masonic temple in front of a retail merchants' convention in 1909, that Bert first heard her voice. He was charmed immediately and approached her after the show to compliment her performance, and they made plans to see each other socially. Theirs was a whirlwind romance. They were both genuinely smitten with each other. Their personalities and abilities complemented each other well, so after a short courtship of a few months, they married at the Methodist church in Guthrie. He was thirty and she was twenty-six, making them older than most newlyweds of their time.

For the first twenty years of their marriage, Della was not actively involved in the operation of the store. She certainly learned about merchandise during the buying trips she and Bert took several times each year to New York and Europe, and she no doubt served as Bert's close confidant on business decisions. But there isn't any evidence to suggest that she took charge of any store duties or managed any departments. Where Della excelled, of course, was in entertaining their guests in a grand style befitting the owners of the state's largest department store and as a charming companion to the many social functions Bert was obligated to attend. As one would expect, their home at 301 Northwest Eighteenth Street was a showplace of elegant furnishings. Functions at the Brown home were always circled on social calendars around the city.

In the early 1930s, the Browns' close friend G.A. "Doc" Nichols, who had built their home on Northwest Eighteenth Street, convinced them to build one of the first homes in his new Nichols Hills country club development north of the Oklahoma City limits at Northwest Sixty-Third and Western Streets. Bert had just begun his ascendancy as one of the city's business and philanthropic leaders, and this impressive new home seemed to cement his position.

An unfortunate side effect of Bert's reputation as a leader in the community came in 1933. In July, an ambitious bootlegger-turned-gangster from Memphis, George "Machine Gun" Kelly, and an accomplice kidnapped the Browns' former neighbor Charles Urschel as he played bridge on a back porch of his home at 400 Northwest Eighteenth Street.

The Brown House on Guilford Lane in Nichols Hills became known for lavish parties and society fêtes, 1932. *Oklahoma Historical Society, the Gateway to Oklahoma History.*

Kelly had been recently made unemployed by the end of Prohibition and had turned to bank robbing and other easy methods of earning cash during the Depression. He was not nearly as fierce as his nickname, invented by his wife essentially as a marketing brand for media coverage, would have you believe; in fact, she had to purchase a surplus Thompson machine gun from a pawn shop to flesh out the nickname, as Kelly was not a particularly violent criminal.

As such, he wasn't much of a kidnapper either. After ten days of captivity, Urschel was released when a $200,000 ransom had been paid. But Urschel observed many details of his captivity, and his information led the FBI to the Kelly gang fairly quickly. Kelly and his wife were arrested in Memphis in September. Their trial was held in Oklahoma City in October.

During the trial, testimony revealed that the Kelly gang had considered several people before deciding on Urschel, who was selected because they felt an oilman would've been able to raise the cash more quickly than other prominent people. Among the men they had considered kidnapping were John A. Brown and his good friend Frank Johnson of the First National Bank. Because word had gotten out that Bert was a potential target, because their friend and former neighbor had been taken and because the kidnappers had later been near her new home, Della developed an idea in her mind that Bert had been in eminent danger of abduction. Her fear was only confirmed when she learned that Johnson had also thwarted a threatened abduction of his grandchildren.

This fear of harm stalked Della for the rest of her life. She shrank from public life. Parties at the Brown mansion were rare after that. Bert began attending charity functions without his charming companion. Only during their buying trips was Della out in public for any great length of time. After Bert's untimely death, some close to the couple even suggested that the strain caused by the empathy he felt for his wife diminished his health, and though that was not an official diagnosis, his sudden death despite the appearance of good health confirmed the belief for those who held it.

Despairing over Bert's passing, Della confided to friends that she did not see how she could possibly carry on his work at the store. However, a few days after Bert's funeral, Della met with the management of the store to discuss the future of the company. Brown's comptroller Laura Ambrose assured her that the company had solid business plans for the next few months. She had no doubt that the faithful and able people with whom Mr. Brown had labored for many years would be able to continue store operations for the foreseeable future. With sincere frankness, Ambrose told Della that she did not see how she could *not* carry on Bert's work at the store.

And so, heeding the counsel of those closest to her and realizing that there is no better therapy than work, Della Dunkin Brown decided to move forward. With Laura Ambrose by her side, Della would eventually surpass even Bert Brown's level of success and become one of the most powerful Oklahoma City business leaders of her time.

6

"Welcome to Brown's!"

Over the weeks and months following John A. Brown's death, Della Dunkin Brown began to spend more time at the store, taking a firmer grip on the reins. A neighbor remarked that Della had "gone into a shell when Mr. Brown died. She gradually began dropping from the city's social life and devoted her entire life to the business. When I asked her about it she told me, 'It isn't any fun to be a widow, so I'm going to become a businesswoman.'" Longtime family friend and business partner Eliot Lyon was not surprised at all when Della showed business prowess. He had known Della since before she had even met Bert; his siblings had taken music lessons from her in Guthrie. "Although a woman in every sense of the word," he said, "she was much like a man—she was quite opinionated."

Within a year of taking over the business, Della and vice-president Laura Ambrose embarked on an aggressive expansion program in the Oklahoma City area. Brown's was already playing catch-up of a sort as another one of downtown's big three retailers, Kerr's, had already opened a small shop on Varsity Corner (now Campus Corner) in Norman in 1936 and a suburban store, Kerr's Uptown, at Northwest Twenty-Fourth and Walker Streets in 1937. Indeed, risk-taking was one of the most obvious differences between the two stores. While Brown's certainly made innovations in merchandising and promotion, Kerr's was always the more adventurous when it came to expansion. The mindset at Brown's was to endeavor to do something the best, if not the first.

Right: Seemingly overnight, Della Dunkin Brown went from merchant's wife to the most powerful woman in Oklahoma retail. *Courtesy of the Oklahoma Historical Society.*

Below: The Brown's College Corner location at 323 West Boyd Street opened in 1941. It was the first store closed when Dillard's took over. *Courtesy of the Oklahoma Historical Society.*

Brown's opened its own Norman store, Brown's College Corner, on the northeast corner of Boyd and Buchanan Streets in 1941. The new store marketed primarily to college students and, as such, stocked mainly clothing, but any Brown's merchandise could be shipped to College Corner. A new delivery route was added between downtown and Norman.

The college girl was the main customer of Brown's College Corner. The "co-ed," as college girls were called, was a new tour de force in the marketing world as women began to attend public universities in large numbers for the first time in the late 1930s and early 1940s. Generally, the marketing was centered on fashion and the supposition that young women only attended college to earn the "MRS degree"—that is, to catch a husband. The first year the Norman store was open, Brown's College Corner ran an ad in the *Sooner Yearbook* designed to appeal to the typical co-ed.

That same year, Brown's debuted two other services geared to the college female customer: Brown's College Council and *Brown's Time for Charm*. For the college council, Brown's recruited a dozen young women from local and national colleges to act as fashion consultants and personal shoppers for the discerning female student. Though such a service seems somewhat elitist, it jibed with Brown's steadfast mission to provide exceptional service at an exceptional value:

> *Twelve on-their-toes gals whose chief interest in life is to pack you off to college with the just-right-clothes you want. Twelve gals who know what's right because they've been there. They'll tell you all the must-have's and nice-to-have's and guide you within a budget that will make pappy happy and goad him into buying you a few glamorous extras.*

Brown's Time for Charm was a radio program on WKY along the lines of the Marilyn Arbee personal shopper program. In *Time for Charm*, Carolyn Brown presented helpful advice to young women on varying topics like fashion, grooming, jewelry and even dating. As it was broadcast over the air, it was certainly open to everyone, but Brown's marketed it to the interest of the young, single woman.

Della made another move toward growth in 1941 when she acquired a six-story warehouse at 214 Northwest Second Street, due north of the main store. The location was beneficial for Brown's in the sense that the additional storage allowed them to display more merchandise in the main store, but downtown was already becoming very crowded and having the large Brown's delivery trucks blocking streets, sidewalks and alleys in two

This 1941 ad from the *Sooner Yearbook* illustrates the intended goal of some co-ed students at the time. *The University of Oklahoma,* Sooner Yearbook.

places downtown only intensified a burgeoning parking and traffic crisis.

Della continued to expand Brown's Downtown footprint, acquiring more floor space in three buildings on the First Street side between 1943 and 1947. This left Brown's in occupation of the entire street front of First Street and of all but the two corner buildings on Main. Obtaining and using the Perrine or Hales building storefronts on Robinson was out of the question, but the Alexander Drug warehouse on the corner of First and Harvey Streets was attractive, especially since Brown's already occupied the storefront and basement there.

In the meantime, Della cast an eye to the south when looking to expand. Oklahoma City's south side had been largely overlooked by businessmen and developers since the city's founding. Kerr's had already moved into Uptown, and there were not really any other suitable locations under development on the north side at that time. So Della opted to accept Capitol Hill developer L.M. Rauch's offer to occupy his large three-story building at 321 West Commerce (Southwest Twenty-Fifth) Street in 1948. Brown's stood in the center of the north side of the street between Harvey and Hudson. To the east was a space later occupied by a JCPenney. One door west was Allen's 5-10-25 Cents Store (with Brown's furniture department occupying the two floors above), and on the corner of Commerce and Hudson was Katz Drug. A decade later, Brown's and Katz's north side counterparts would figure mightily in the city's civil rights history. Similar to the Norman store, the Capitol Hill store offered a narrower range of merchandise geared to its customer base, but any product could be delivered from downtown.

That same year, Brown's leased the building at 219–21 West First Street and installed a store devoted exclusively to appliances there. This building was in the middle of the block just north of the main store's First Street

The Capitol Hill branch opened on Commerce Street in 1948. When Crossroads Mall opened, this location became administration offices. *Courtesy of the Oklahoma Historical Society.*

entrance and almost directly behind the company warehouse on Second Street. The new store and the warehouse were not connected, however, because in those days Civic Center Park ran the length of the boulevard along Couch Drive between Harvey and Broadway, and there was not an alley there as such. The warehouse, the appliance store and the city park have all since been replaced by the massive Leadership Square complex. Called Brown's Annex, the new store featured appliances, bicycles, auto accessories and a tag agency.

Brown and Ambrose finally secured a long-term lease for the entirety of the Alexander Drug Company building in May 1950, adapting the six-story building to fit into the existing Brown's structure. Most of the earlier expansions involved only first-floor storefronts, which were easy enough to combine with the rest of Brown's street front, but for this major new addition, the architects had to employ ramps on floors two and three because the two buildings had differing floor heights. They also constructed new covered walkways on the south side of the new building to connect it with the Main Street side of the store. This turned out to be a major renovation once it was finished and increased floor space by about 36 percent. In comparison, the original store had twelve thousand square feet with a twenty-five-foot storefront on Main Street, making it the smallest department store in the city in its day. Now Brown's spilled over ten acres with storefronts on Main, First, Robinson and Harvey Streets. At its maximum development, the building varied in height from one to six stories and was a veritable labyrinth of merchandise.

When finished, the new store represented the pinnacle of downtown shopping in Oklahoma City. The decade between 1945 and 1955 is the golden era that older residents recall so fondly and the more sentimental of younger Oklahoma Cityans look to as the embodiment of what was lost to urban renewal in the 1960s and 1970s. This was the time when Main Street was teeming with shoppers moving up and down the blocks from Broadway to Walker Street. Most major stores could be found on Main Street—Brown's, Kerr's, Halliburton's, Montgomery Ward and Penney's were all there—although the Sears, Roebuck was located on Grand Avenue. Other favorites on Main were boutique stores like Rothschild's, Kamber's, Peyton-Marcus and Virginia Dare; drugstores like Katz and Walgreen; and the Kress and Woolworth dime stores. You could purchase almost any consumer product short of boats and automobiles in the district, and even those could possibly be purchased in a catalogue store.

In those days, Main Street shopping at the big stores could be as much a social event as anything else. Some shoppers dressed sharply when they set out on buying excursions. Men would wear suits, and women would wear dresses, white gloves and hats. Brown's was a destination, and shoppers marveled at the sheer size of the place as much as the exotic merchandise from all around the world and the curiosities you didn't see every day. And Brown's encouraged this "retail tourism."

Several new features were added to the John A. Brown store during the renovation that secured its position as a destination shopping place. The most remarkable new feature was the set of escalators between the first and third floors, touted as Oklahoma City's first escalators:

> *Tomorrow, Saturday, begins Fair Week, the Great State Fair with its wonderful exhibits and spectacular entertainment. You will want to come to Brown's during your visit to see and ride our new escalators from the first floor to the third floor and down again. Only the young in heart like ourselves can understand the joys of escalator escapades. Here at the John A. Brown Company is a streamlined stairway express that transports you through an almost endless wonderland of fascinating merchandise.*

During the state fair, thousands of people would pass through Brown's doors daily. *From the* Daily Oklahoman.

Here in one complete store unfolds the story of never ceasing tours of the world's marts...a never ending quest in search of merchandise of merit. We are constantly striving to bring you the finest in quality...assortments... and values. Here under one roof is surprise...enchantment...excitement. And here at Brown's we are endeavoring day-in and day-out to make our escalators the best ride in town...and all for free too.

There was also a nurse's station that served both employees and customers alike and was staffed by a professional nurse. Considering there could be over one thousand people in the store at any given time, this was a prudent move by the store, and the nurse—in starched white uniform, cap, hose and shoes—dealt with all manner of first aid situations. Velma Fehse was the nurse for many years and was called Bubbles around the store because of her vibrant personality.

The additional space also allowed room for more services. Watch repair and shoe repair shops were added. The mail and telephone order service was booming just as much as traditional shopping, and the volume had become so much that the U.S. Postal Service added a window in Brown's that could serve the public and the store. Brown's received orders from all over Oklahoma and countries in all six inhabited continents. Many of the mail orders were addressed to Marilyn Arbee and often would include a Christmas shopping list with the names of people, their gender and age and their shipping addresses. The store would select, wrap and mail the packages at no extra charge beyond shipping. By this time, of course, Marilyn Arbee was the embodiment of the mail order department, which included dozens of employees and five telephone operators.

To help with the load, the renovation featured a new telephone switchboard that allowed an operator in the mail order department to accept a call from a customer and patch in a clerk from the sales floor; the customer and clerk discussed the merchandise and the operator took the order all in the same conversation. The switchboard also introduced the paging system with the familiar chimes so many customers remember even today. Different tones signaled various employees or departments to contact the operator from the nearest phone.

Obviously, all the mail order and delivery traffic made the alley in the center of the building rather chaotic. Brown's had taken to referring to it as the "Busiest Alley in America." The alley ran east–west between Robinson and Harvey Avenues, and a steady stream of vehicles flowed through at all times of day. There were walkways above for the upper floors, but on street

Just another busy day at Brown's, 1960s. *Oklahoma Images, Metropolitan Library System.*

level, an employee was posted there to act as both doorman and crossing guard to ensure customers could safely pass from the Main Street to the First Street sections. This was mitigated for the most part when the renovation added new walkways above and a fully interconnected basement below.

The basement store was the largest basement store in the southwest and one of the largest in country. It originally sold irregular, discontinued or damaged merchandise, but the new basement was heralded as a "store within a store" because there were the same departments as on the upper floors—clothing for the entire family, shoes and housewares and domestics—but the merchandise was similar to what one would find at a discount store. It had its own store manager and its own buyers and existed as an almost separate entity.

The most important thing that distinguished the basement from the rest of the store was a large luncheonette. Brown's had had a soda fountain since the Brock's days, but this new installation included a soda fountain and added a lunch counter with additional seating in booths. The luncheonette was in the center of the basement and was visible from the upper store by a cutout in the floor that was hemmed in by railing. They didn't know it in 1952, but before the decade was out, the luncheonette was destined to be at the center of something else entirely—the civil rights movement in Oklahoma City

7
"Record Days"

Throughout the 1950s, Della Brown improved the John A. Brown Company's place in the commercial and business life of Oklahoma City. The postwar expansion had given the store a larger physical presence in downtown, and the company had made its first expansion out of the central business district by looking south, first to Norman and then to Capitol Hill. It had also secured its place in the hearts and pocketbooks of Oklahoma shoppers and successfully held its own against the influx of large national retailers into downtown in the 1930s and proudly changed its slogan to "Oklahoma Born—Oklahoma Owned—Oklahoma Managed."

The massive downtown John A. Brown store truly represented the apex of retail shopping in the city center when it was finished in 1952, but the cracks were already forming that would bring about the ultimate collapse of downtown retail and John A. Brown's. The problems began in the postwar 1940s, when several factors combined to complicate downtown business patterns. As manufacturers around the country returned to peacetime production of consumer goods and wartime price controls and rationing went away, retail demand grew, and Main Street swelled with shoppers. Auto manufacturers switched from producing military vehicles to personal automobiles, and in Oklahoma City, the streetcar system had been purchased, dismantled and replaced with a bus system, which provided less coverage. Downtown areas across the nation were not equipped to handle this influx of automobiles, so traffic often snarled into gridlock.

This rare interior shot shows the quality merchandise and surroundings that kept Brown's competitive, 1956. *Photo by Dick Peterson; Oklahoma Historical Society, the Gateway to Oklahoma History.*

Downtown landowners, many of them residing out of state, responded by demolishing buildings, paving the empty lots and converting them to parking. One notable example was the massive castle-like Oklahoma County Courthouse off Main Street in the block between Dewey and Walker adjacent to the Montgomery Ward building. Another was the conversion of the large central streetcar terminal into a surface parking lot on the northeast corner of Hudson and Grand (Sheridan) Streets. Parking rates were inflated as well, prompting at least two investigations by city authorities after allegations of price gouging were made. There were a few garages constructed, but lot owners could turn a larger profit (a 1948 news article suggested it was a 500 percent increase in income) by razing a building and paving the lot, despite the inefficiency it represented for the overall downtown community. The net effect of increased shoppers, increased cars and increased parking rates was that the consumer was becoming disgruntled with Main Street shopping.

The first retailer to fold its downtown tent was the big Sears store on Grand Street. Sears had never really been fully committed to urban core retail stores. This was certainly true in Oklahoma City, as Sears arrived later than other stores and did not select a Main Street location. Around 1950, the national leadership initiated the policy of removing most Sears stores out of the nation's downtown areas and into the suburbs. In 1951, an eleven-acre site (larger than Brown's footprint) in Oklahoma City on the northwest corner of Northwest Twenty-Third and Pennsylvania Streets was secured from Clyde Shepherd, who owned a farm along the north side of Northwest Twenty-Third between Penn and Villa Streets.

The big Sears store was finally completed in spring of 1954, making such a clean break from downtown that the company even closed the original store a few weeks before the new one was opened and paid out a three-year lease on the vacant building. With maps showing all major routes into the city converging smoothly into the new location, Sears ads proudly boasted that the store offered everything a downtown store could not:

Shopping downtown had its many joys, but slogging through cold rain was not one of them, as this 1954 photo shows. *Photo by Dick Peterson; Oklahoma Historical Society, the Gateway to Oklahoma History.*

> *Free Parking! Room for 750 cars! No parking troubles here! No tickets! No meters! No charge of any kind to park your car—stay as long as you wish.*
>
> *Smooth Escalators! No more slow, crowded elevators! Safe, efficient escalators to speed you on your way—no tiresome waiting for elevators here. Escalators on every floor.*
>
> *NEW! super service station! Allstate gasoline, oil, tires, seat covers and auto accessories! DRIVE IN—have your car serviced as you "browse" and see our NEW STORE!*
>
> *NEW! it's air conditioned. You'll enjoy every minute spent in SEARS NEW STORE! Every floor, every department is completely air conditioned for your shopping comfort!*

Downtown shopping would survive for another twenty years, but Sears began the slow exodus out to the suburbs as newer and bigger shopping centers were developed. In 1953, JCPenney installed a new store in developer C.B. Warr's Mayfair Shopping Center at Northwest Fiftieth and May Streets, joining another downtown name, Rothschild's. On the south side, Sylvan N. Goldman attracted Kerr's to the Reding Shopping Center at Southwest Forty-Fourth and May. The biggest new development to come along in the 1950s, though, was the Belleview Shopping Center (later Penn Square) created by Ben Wileman. The passing of Anton Classen's widow, Ella, created the opportunity. Ella Classen inherited the Classen Companies from her husband after his early passing in 1922. She controlled large swathes of land and indirectly guided the city planning and development process because of land that she would or would not sell for development. The best example of this was the Classen dairy farm adjacent to the west of Belle Isle Park. Highly sought after for years because of its prime location alongside the U.S. 66 bypass and the Northwest Highway and nestled on the southern border of the lucrative Nichols Hills demographic, Ella Classen had succeeded in keeping her husband's cherished farm not only out of development but also out of the city limits, even keeping Pennsylvania Avenue from traversing the area for many years. After Classen's passing in 1955, Wileman was able to obtain the farmland. In 1957, he built the Belle Isle residential subdivision to the west of Penn and north of Northwest Highway and in 1958 the fifty-five-acre Belleview Shopping Center on the east side of Penn.

Wileman easily convinced Montgomery Ward to build the largest store in the chain there, and he naturally looked to "Oklahoma's Greatest Store" for the other anchor. Della eagerly signed with Wileman. Already dealing with an earlier crisis at Brown-Dunkin in Tulsa, she was unaware that another crisis in downtown Oklahoma City was just beginning that would strain her abilities as a leader and permanently tarnish the legacy of the John A. Brown Company.

Despite early doubters, Della Dunkin Brown proved to be more than capable of running the company her husband had built and essentially doubled it in size and sales volume through her own efforts. Still, despite her success as a businesswoman, she never quite became the formidable force she could have been. She was not in the leadership of the Oklahoma City Chamber of Commerce like her husband, John A. Brown. She was not on the board of any other major companies or banks. There were also routine exhibitions of sexism, especially in the media, such as sending junior female reporters to interview her, usually about her views on fashion or travel, and often sticking to the policy of referring to a woman by her husband's name (i.e., Mrs. John A. Brown). Often her accomplishments were dismissed as being those of her husband.

It would be easy to ascribe this lack of power and influence to being a woman in a man's world, but the truth is that the reclusiveness that Della exhibited while Bert was alive only intensified after he was gone and as her position became more prominent. It undoubtedly hampered her ability to take a greater role in the affairs of the city. The reclusiveness became an ingrained part of Della's very identity to the point that she eventually referred to herself as D.D. Brown in business correspondence and requested that reporters use the name in news items and press releases. They did so only occasionally. When the *Daily Oklahoman* asked her for biographical information that it could keep on file for future stories, she sent the blank form back to them with a polite note stating her unwillingness to draw attention to herself. After her death, the paper's business columnist J. Willis Baker recalled that he once asked her to write a guest column for him. At the last minute, she called his office and frantically asked him not to run the piece because she was afraid of attracting attention to herself. Of course, men in business often used only initials, and it's possible that she chose to use initials as a defense against being prejudged because of her gender. But when examined as a whole alongside anecdotes like those above and others, such as entering hospitals and making donations under assumed names, it seems her fear of abduction or physical harm always guided her actions.

Outside the executive suite of the downtown store, where she dealt almost exclusively with Laura Ambrose and the other vice-presidents, Della was rarely seen in public in Oklahoma City. She lived alone in the immense home at 1601 Guilford Lane and even the attendants—the gardener, chauffeur and other servants—were not residents of the house. Her personal companion, forty-something divorcée Essie Harp, shared the same address, and the two traveled together, though Harp ostensibly lived in the cabana at the rear of the house. The only social engagements were occasional holiday meals with John H. Dunkin's family from Tulsa.

John H. Dunkin had forged a career in Tulsa that would have made Bert Brown proud. The Brown-Dunkin store had achieved a regional ascendancy similar to that of its big sister store in Oklahoma City, and Dunkin was a powerful figure on the Tulsa scene. He expanded the store from its three-story building and seventy employees to eighteen floors of merchandise spread over three buildings with more than eight hundred employees. He served in leadership roles for the Tulsa Chamber of Commerce, the National Retail Dry Goods Association and several civic and charitable organizations and was the spokesman for Senator Robert S. Kerr's campaign for a navigable Arkansas River. On the evening of June 12, 1958, he went home from the office and, shortly after, died from a heart attack despite his apparent good health and lack of complaints about illness. He was sixty-six.

Although she couldn't have known it at the time, her brother's death came at an inopportune time for Della. Already in the midst of negotiating with Wileman over the Belleview project, she found it too great a burden to run the Tulsa store, and her sister-in-law, Jane Randolph Dunkin, was not up to the task of running it either (though Jane would be described as a businesswoman and philanthropist years later). The two heirs of the Brown-Dunkin store handed the management of the store to W.R. Chappell, who had been Dunkin's protégé in Tulsa for the past fifteen years and who had just returned from working in a store in Charlotte, North Carolina, to round out his executive experience. The two women reorganized the company and created the D and J Investment Company to manage their Tulsa properties.

In August, ten days after the deal with Ben Wileman was inked, a young African American teacher named Clara Luper entered the Katz Drug Store on the southwest corner of Main and Robinson Streets with thirteen children from the NAACP Youth Council, sat at the lunch counter and asked to be served. The manager initially refused to serve them, but he dutifully conferred with the national office of the company in Kansas City. After two days, the children returned for a third day and were served their orders just

Sit-ins in Oklahoma City also affected the high-profile John A. Brown luncheonette. The organizer, Clara Luper, later became a dear friend of Della's. Image from 1958. *Oklahoma Historical Society, the Gateway to Oklahoma History*.

like any other customer. With that, Katz became the first store downtown to integrate. Veazey's and Kress announced they were open to all customers the next day.

Emboldened by their success, Luper and thirty-five children ranging in age from six to seventeen entered John A. Brown's downtown store intent on integrating the luncheonette in the basement. Luper later admitted that she selected Brown's next not only because of its status as "Oklahoma's Greatest Store" but also because she thought they would be welcomed at the luncheonette. She knew that Brown's had been one of the few stores that welcomed African American customers, and many in the community appreciated Bert's liberal credit policy and willingness to hire African American employees. That's not to say that Brown's did not have certain Jim Crow policies—there were separate restrooms, and blacks were not allowed to try on clothing, ride in elevators or eat in the luncheonette or tearoom—but Brown's had otherwise always extended Bert's policy of generosity and friendliness to all customers regardless of race. The African American community had likewise responded by giving the store the majority of its trade.

Luper's faith in Brown's was not rewarded. She and the children entered Brown's and descended the stairs to the luncheonette. Luper noticed that the same clerks who had always waited on her cheerfully before were slack-jawed when they saw the group silently walk in and go downstairs. "One clerk stuck out her tongue at me and made an ugly face," she wrote in her book *Behold the Walls*. "Am I in John A. Brown's, or in a Lion's Den?" she asked out loud. One of the children remarked, "Mrs. Luper, we aren't in the Lion's Den. I think that we are in Hell."

The staff at the luncheonette counter refused to serve them, so the children quietly sat as the older ones read books and magazines and the younger ones colored pages with crayons. The group stayed until closing and left without incident, but they came back every day for the next ten days; tensions began to rise. Frank Wade held the contract with Brown's to operate the luncheonette. He was well known in eateries downtown and operated at least a dozen cafés, including the Cigar Store for over forty years. Wade dug in and refused to serve the protesters.

As the days turned into weeks, the protests continued. The children began to refer to Wade as Uncle Frank and his two employees as Aunt Francis and Aunt Mildred. Brown's became the focal point of the civil rights movement in Oklahoma City—or, as Luper called it, the Bunker Hill. The protesters, still mainly children, were spat on, shouted at, pushed over, cursed at and even punched. The Oklahoma City Police Department was there every day, as well, but only to enforce order and did not take action against anyone who was not disturbing the peace. At times, as many as 150 children participated in the sit-in at the luncheonette while white customers created obstructions, such as only giving up seats to other white people. Wade reserved some tables for employees only and removed the chairs from others.

Unsurprisingly, Della Brown receded from the controversy. Luper received poison letters, death threats and bomb scares at her home. It can be assumed that Della Brown must have taken that news with some measure of terror, although there's no record of her reaction only her complete silence. Her silence and unwillingness to show strong leadership during the crisis ultimately weakened Brown's. The company that was built on providing the gold standard in customer service to all was now acting hypocritically by refusing service to some. What's worse, the store's reputation was damaged by the policies of contracted workers, not Brown's employees.

A few days after the protests heated up, a letter to the editor appeared in the *Black Dispatch* newspaper from Caroline Burks, a retired white schoolteacher who was a pioneer settler in the county. The following letter was addressed to Mrs. John A. Brown and Kermit Hardwick, the general manager:

> *Dear Madam and Sir:*
>
> *I enjoy shopping at Brown's and am sorry to have to withdraw my patronage and moral support from this store, but I will not spend my money with any concern that is so un-Christian, so undemocratic as you have proved to be by discriminating against our Negro citizens. Withholding my*

money will not break your store but withdrawal of my moral support may be consequential.

Do you think Negroes will patronize John Brown Co. after these recent insults? I know many white people who won't.

The rudeness of those waitresses to those fine young men and women shows the level to which white trash can sink. But perhaps they were trained to act as they did…

With regrets,

Caroline E.M. Burks
Retired Educator B.S., M.A., Columbia University

Burks was spot on with her assessment. The events at Brown's were a topic for daily conversation all around town, by the water cooler and over the fence. Some shoppers did avoid the store for a while, especially African Americans. In *Behold the Walls*, Luper recounts a conversation she had with a couple who had come to check on the safety of their granddaughter: "The man spoke first. He said that every time his wife went downtown, she'd always go to John A. Brown's to shop. 'Yes, Brown's has everything; I especially like the hats and their clearance sales are terrific,' the lady said. 'Every month my charge account is sky high. Now look at us, and here's my seven-year-old grandchild standing down here in the one store where I have spent my salary as fast as Tinker Field could pay me.'" It was this sense of betrayal that strengthened the resolve of the protesters and is still remembered today by many African Americans in Oklahoma City.

Over the next year, the protesters expanded the sit-ins to several other businesses downtown but never let up the pressure on John A. Brown's. Other downtown restaurants were encouraged by Wade's resistance at the luncheonette and they dug in as well. These included the city's most beloved cafeteria, Anna Maude's, in the basement of the Cravens Building (Robinson Renaissance today), Bishop's on Broadway and the Forum Cafeteria on Park. At times, they were too vocal or obstructive. Luper and others were jailed for disturbing the peace, but they were always quickly released on bond.

By the spring of 1961, the protests had been going on for two and a half years when a new group of protesters, predominantly white students and professors from the University of Oklahoma, began picketing the Brown's College Corner store in Norman. Students from Oklahoma City University and area secondary schools performed a mock funeral with hearse and motorcade. They gave silent prayer vigils. Even actor Charlton Heston, fresh from the set of the epic *El Cid* and in town visiting his good friend Dr. L.J. West, took part in the demonstrations during Memorial Day weekend.

Despite the stubbornness and tenacity of their resistance to integration, Della Brown, Frank Wade and the other restaurant owners found the tide turning that summer. Events like sit-ins in Greensboro, North Carolina, and the violent attacks on the Freedom Riders in Alabama were drawing national attention, and in Oklahoma, Governor Edmondson created a commission to address civil rights issues in 1960.

Finally, in June, 1961, Clara Luper "received an emergency call" asking if she would visit the store immediately to speak with Mrs. Brown. Luper recalled how she had been asking to speak to Della Brown since 1957 and had received no response—not even "no," just nothing. On the phone with Brown's office, her mind raced, and she thought, "After all she has done to me…she has nerve…the nerve of her telling me to come down immediately." She spoke into the phone, "No, I shall not talk to Mrs. Brown—thank you for calling, but now I'm busy—too busy." Luper spent the next day consulting with her family and her advisors and the sit-inners themselves. Every one she spoke to told her to talk to Della Brown.

Luper relented and agreed to meet Della a week later. She refused the offer of a chauffeured ride to the store and drove herself to the meeting. On arrival, she felt tension all through the store as she made her way to the offices. She re-created the historic moment in *Behold the Walls*:

> *That day I was ready for Mrs. John A. Brown. All of the frustrations that had been building in me for the last four years were going to come out "right in her white face."*
>
> *When the secretary opened the door, I walked into an office. I was overcome with history because that office was Mr. John A. Brown's former office. The furniture, the pictures, the papers and in spite of the improvements and re-furnishings that had happened at John A. Brown's, that office was just as it was when Mr. John A. Brown died years ago. My frustrations began to diminish and when Mrs. Brown opened the door we both stood speechless before each other with tears in our eyes, we embraced each other as if we had been friends for years. Oh, I know this couldn't be, but it was, and now we were talking. Two women, one black and one white. One rich and one poor.*
>
> *Historical circumstances had brought us together. We talked about our families and some of the problems that we had faced as we both tried to*

compete in a man's business world. We both cried again as I told her how I tried to make it. How I was working on three jobs trying to educate my children and to provide them with the necessities of life. She told me about her husband and how he had died. We talked about how much we had loved and how much we had lost.

Finally, she said, "I have I been told that you hate me, is that true?" I said, "No, Mrs. Brown. I do not hate you. I respect you. You have challenged the male-oriented business world, you shall always have my respect."

"I have been told that you hated me," I said.

"Oh, no, Clara, I've heard that, but it is not true. I admire your courage. I have stood here and wondered day in and day out, what you and your children were saying about me. Clara tell me, please tell me, what the children think about me? What do they say, Clara?"

As I looked at her, I knew that I had to tell her the truth. Her penetrating eyes stared directly into mine.

"Mrs. Brown, they say that they wish you had died in place of Mr. John A. Brown. They said if he were living they believe that they would be able to eat here," I said.

For a few minutes there was complete silence and then she spoke.

"Clara, day in and day out, I have worried about this thing. I just don't know how to deal with it. You see, Mr. Frank Wade has leased space in my store to operate the luncheonette and under his lease he has the sole right to run it in his own way. You see my hands have been completely tied."

"Yes, Mrs. Brown, but we don't know anything about Frank Wade and care less, but John A. Brown's that's different. This is the store where we have spent our money and we can't see how we can be discriminated against under the roof of a John A. Brown store. Even the name John Brown reminds us of the martyr that died for our cause."

We talked for nearly an hour. Mr. Anderson came in and brought us some lemonade. He offered her the first glass and she said, "Serve Clara first."

Finally she said, "Take this message back to the children. Segregation will end at John A. Brown's."

I was so proud of her. She admitted to me that the first time I was arrested, she called and offered to pay my bond. She never missed calling to see if I were all right, she said.

She asked me to do her a favor. To come and meet with all of the executives of the John A. Brown's store and tell them why we selected John A. Brown's Store.

I followed her to a spacious conference room where I told my story. I liked everybody there immediately except Attorney [Lytle]. *He continued to harass me about insignificant things. I had already been warned about him. I started to raise my voice at him, but I looked at Mrs. Brown and she smiled at me. Then, I knew everything was going to be alright* [sic].

When I left John A. Brown's that day, I had respect for Miss [Ambrose], *Mr. Hardwick, and I knew, I had a life time friend in Mrs. John A. Brown.*

An agreement was made that day that John A. Brown's Segregation Walls would fall and in less than a week, blacks were eating at John A. Brown's.

Mrs. Brown and I continued to talk to each other by telephone. She invited me to go to Europe with her. I turned it down because of other commitments and before she went into the hospital for the last time, she called me and told me she was going into the hospital under a different name and she probably would never see me again, but she wanted me to know that she appreciated what we had done for this city, a city she loved so well.

Mrs. John A. Brown acquainted me with loneliness in a way that I had never known it before.

8

"Oklahoma Born, Oklahoma Owned, Oklahoma Managed"

The civil rights protests did not substantially harm John A. Brown's business. For the most part, protesters were quite orderly and did not accost shoppers entering or leaving the store. Inside the sprawling downtown store, the sit-ins were confined to the basement store, and there were no reports that the disturbances dissuaded shoppers from visiting the store. The real harm done was to the legacy of the store, certainly among African Americans, but also among an increasing number of students and historians who know the store only through the lens of the civil rights movement and not as "Oklahoma's Greatest Store."

If anything drew business away from the big John A. Brown store downtown during the civil rights period, it was the new sister store at the Penn Square Shopping Center which opened in 1960. The chamber of commerce and the media outlets heavily promoted the center, calling it a "city within a city" and saying things like the mall signaled "the arrival of Oklahoma City as a metropolitan city." A lot of the coverage involved superlatives—1.6 million bricks, 4.4 million pounds of steel, three hundred miles of wiring, enough cement to build a sidewalk from Oklahoma City to Tulsa—and one particular, if mild, jab at the downtown merchants: if the covered walkways were placed end-to-end on Main Street, they would stretch from Broadway to Western Avenue, a fine thing since Main Street shopping was only three blocks long and few of the sidewalks were covered.

Wileman worked with the noted city architecture firm Sorey, Hill & Sorey and venerable Tulsa building firm Manhattan Construction to

The new store at Penn Square had many of the amenities of the downtown store. Best of all, perhaps, was the plentiful free parking. *Oklahoma Historical Society, the Gateway to Oklahoma History*.

Penn Square Mall, circa late 1970s. *Oklahoma Historical Society, the Gateway to Oklahoma History*.

devise a campus-style pedestrian mall design featuring six buildings. Four of the buildings housed the large anchor stores, and the others housed small boutiques. The one outlier, a seventh building, was Montgomery Ward's Auto Center, which was in the parking area to the southeast. Unlike the strip centers in the city, the storefronts in the new mall faced one another and were connected by a forty-eight-foot-wide concrete walkway to create an outdoor area free of automobile traffic. The anchor stores did have entrances into the parking area, but their main entrances all faced the interior.

Calm and peaceful was the aim of Sorey, Hill & Sorey. Trees and "restful greenery" lined the walkways and entrances. Many of the plants were seasonal and were rotated accordingly—tropicals like date palms and banana trees in the summer and chrysanthemums and poinsettias in the winter. There were twenty thousand tulips in bloom at Easter. A burbling lighted fountain splashed in the northeast corner. Nowhere could you find the bright, flashing neon illumination found downtown; only store names were lighted, and those were dimly backlit.

A "town square" was installed on the east end to be used for fashion shows, concerts or people watching. During the holidays, the mall erected a towering Christmas tree believed to be the largest in the Southwest. Many city residents remember the mammoth tree as a sort of beacon during the holidays, as most of its seven-story height could be seen poking out through the open-air mall and into the sky before Penn Square was enclosed in 1982. Some years, Santa Claus arrived by helicopter on the roof of Montgomery Ward and then had breakfast with children in John A. Brown's restaurant.

When completed, Penn Square included forty-six stores. Montgomery Ward was the southeast anchor. It was the largest Ward's store west of Detroit and the third largest in the five-hundred-plus store chain. The northeast anchor was a Humpty Dumpty supermarket. On the northwest corner was Rothschild's, an upscale clothing store from downtown, though smaller by half than the other anchors. On the southwest corner was John A. Brown's. Medium- and small-sized stores salted the rest of the big center, including Oklahoma City's first S.S. Kresge discount store and local chains like Street's, Cutchall's, Peyton-Marcus, May Brothers and Parks. For the weary shopper, ValGene's Restaurant offered a prototype food court like those common in modern shopping malls. Under a single roof and operated by restaurateurs James Vallion and Gene Smelser, who would eventually run some of the most beloved restaurants in city history (e.g., Across the Street, Herman's Seafood), were five food options—the Red Eagle was a fine-dining area with seating for 200, ValGene's Cafeteria served 240 and ValGene's

Coffee Shop sat 70. A basement banquet area and a catering service could handle crowds of up to 500.

Although this was the single largest expansion Brown's had yet made, there were not any particularly new features or services offered in the new store. The Penn Square Brown's was just under half the size of the original downtown store and offered most of the lines available in the big store. The most obvious differences were that Penn Square's basement was dedicated to stock storage, a mail room and the employees' break room rather than a bargain store and a luncheonette. The new store did have a tearoom like the original store. It was called the Apple Blossom Room and played host to many club meetings, modeling shows and visits from Santa Claus and Foreman Scotty.

The Penn Square opening was a rare moment of relief for Della Brown. She was still wrestling with the sit-ins at the downtown store, but another point of pressure had been eased just two days before the Penn Square opening. Brown-Dunkin had struggled since the death of John H. Dunkin in 1957. In just two years, the highly profitable Brown-Dunkin store had wavered and then sunk in debt. Banks holding notes on the store were nervous, and merchandise vendors began refusing credit. In a deal brokered by a St. Louis bank, William T. Dillard purchased Brown-Dunkin from Della Brown and Jane Dunkin on March 1, 1960.

The Penn Square store at Christmastime, 1960s. *Oklahoma Historical Society, the Gateway to Oklahoma History.*

Although she'd shed Brown-Dunkin and resolved the civil rights crisis at the downtown store, Della's relief was short-lived. The problems that had plagued downtown retail since the end of World War II had become acute. Compounding the problem was the city's age; at seventy, the urban core was decaying, and its hodgepodge of low-rise buildings and jagged streets suggested Oklahoma City was not a modern American Sunbelt city like its gleaming peers Dallas and Phoenix. In 1956, a handful of the city's elite, representing the chamber of commerce, large banks and the energy industry, initiated the process of using federal funding earmarked for slum clearance in an effort to address downtown's problems. The intent was to resolve the urban core's issues by using tools like eminent domain; relocation of industry, commercial businesses and residences; and building demolitions to create a blank canvas that would allow urban planners and architects to remake Oklahoma City into a sparkling metropolis.

The chief objection to urban renewal, raised by a number of small businessmen, including 1959 mayoral candidate Everett Curtis, was that eminent domain had been used for public good in the past to create infrastructure improvements like water supply lakes and highways, but government taking private property, clearing the land and selling it to someone else amounted to Robin Hood in reverse—taking from the poor to give to the rich. Della Brown, however, was excited at the proposition because she was beholden to seven different absentee landlords who could command almost any amount of rent from the John A. Brown Company, as it would cripple the big downtown store to lose any piece of the puzzle that was its layout.

In the fall of 1961, Mayor Jim Norick established the Urban Renewal Authority and empowered it to plan and implement Oklahoma City's rebirth. Almost a year later, in October 1962, civic leaders under the separate body Urban Action Foundation, many of them the same men who had begun the urban renewal process, attempted to speed the process by providing private funding to hire noted architect I.M. Pei to provide the vision and plans for redesigning the Central Business District. Pei had already done substantial urban design projects in Cleveland, Philadelphia, Boston and Washington, D.C., and was considered one of the stars of the urban renewal movement.

In the final design in 1964, the major components of Pei's plan included not just commercial towers and modern efficient parking structures but also residential and retail improvements. Pei's plan was built around the superblock, essentially taking four existing city blocks, clearing them and redesigning around one large block made up of the four blocks combined.

Thus, the retail superblock, which Pei considered crucial to the success of the plan, was bounded by Hudson, Park, Robinson and Grand Streets. With the exception of the Cravens Building (now known as Robinson Renaissance) and the Colcord Building, the entire four-block area would be razed with the intention of building the huge three-story Galleria shopping mall with three department store anchors, one of which would be John A. Brown. Main Street between Hudson and Robinson, the heart of the old retail district, would disappear as a street to be resurrected as a glass-covered arcade through the Galleria.

Retail presented the biggest problem for the Pei Plan and civic leaders. Unlike the planned large office and residential towers, which could be built on cleared land before tenants moved in, the retail sector had to remain in business somewhere while the blocks were cleared and the Galleria built, a process that could take five or more years. Pei recommended a rotation approach that would allow part of the Galleria to be built, a Main Street tenant moved, the old store razed and then repeated until stores could be safely and fairly transitioned into their new home. Naturally, John A. Brown would move first, but when Della Brown was informed that Brown's future home was to be in the southeast part of the development on Robinson, she balked. At a meeting of the city planning commission in 1965, her attorney, Roy Lytle, said the proposed site was "not suitable" and informed them Mrs. Brown would move all operations to the suburbs if changes were not made. Curiously, Lytle's comments were left out of the *Daily Oklahoman*'s coverage of the meeting but were reported in its sister paper, *Oklahoma City Times*.

By the time the Pei Plan was adopted by the city council in the autumn of 1965, Della Brown's threat was seen by some as entirely plausible if not inevitable. The Main Street that was once the formidable retail force for the entire city was now an increasingly lonely place for John A. Brown's. Since Sears had left downtown entirely in 1954, nearly seventy-five stores had abandoned the retail district. And it wasn't just the mom-and-pop stores. Mighty pillars had fallen as well. Halliburton's, arguably the first and oldest true department store in the city, closed in 1961.

Shepherd Mall lured JCPenney out of downtown in what the company billed as "the biggest and finest store in the entire national chain." Local Penney's manager Charles Truhitte succinctly summed up the situation plaguing the district. "We are closing the downtown store simply because there is no practical way to use present facilities—or remodel them—for our needs. We could figure no way to get the truck loading docks, warehouse space, and parking for a high-volume store downtown," he said when announcing the move. Penney's opted to move sooner rather than later because the I.M. Pei Plan "with all the dreams is at least five years away—and a retail store can't wait for people to move back to its front doors." In early 1966, Montgomery Ward closed its doors downtown.

As Main Street began to slide into chaos and ruin, Della Brown remained resolute while planning the future. Six months after Kerr's and Ward's left downtown, she journeyed to New York to consult with architects about designing the new downtown store. Ever secretive, when asked by reporters about her plans, she said she intended on making the building "the nicest store in the southwest, if, and when, urban renewal authorities decide to do something, or decide to leave me alone." She dispelled rumors that she had gone to New York to sell the store. "Every time I leave town someone always starts the rumor that we're interested in selling. We're not. I have not approached anyone to sell—and no one has approached me. This store was not for sale when I took it over in 1940, and it is not for sale in 1966. While others have, I'm not running out on downtown—because no one, my people or my customers, have ever run out on me."

Brown's sales were steadily increasing, however slight. It continued to remain competitive with the large national chains in merchandising and even added an auto and tire center on the southwest corner of Northwest Thirty-Ninth and Pennsylvania Streets, about one mile south of the Penn Square store, in 1966. Brown's also began to offer an increasing number of services to complement its wide-ranging product lines. In addition to the traditional products it had always offered, the store offered a dizzying array of new services in the 1960s—interior decorating, film developing, picture framing, shoe dying and shoe restyling, an S&H Green Stamp redemption store, magazine subscriptions, stationery printing, monogramming, carpet and installation, a beauty salon, upholstery, television and appliance repair, fur storage and restyling, knitting instruction, silver replating, a wig salon, baby shoe bronzing, old photo restoration, paint and wallpaper, linoleum, bridal consultants and the official Oklahoma City outfitters for Boy and Girl Scouts.

Overall, John A. Brown's corporate health in late 1966 was sound financially, and the company remained robust and competitive. Della Brown, however, was not. She was hospitalized for a time in the autumn of that year, and in September, she revised her will, adding a codicil providing for a trusteeship to operate the store in the event of her incapacitation or demise and a subsequent transition to new ownership. Going into 1967, she was not well at all.

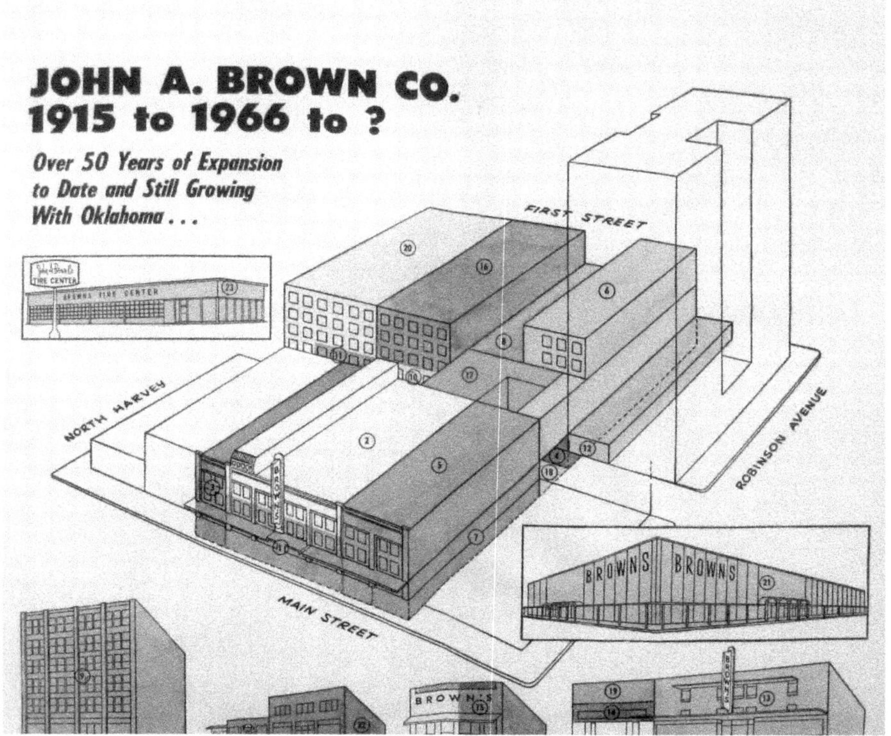

Under Della's strong leadership, Brown's had become an Oklahoma City retail empire encompassing nearly a full block of downtown, a small store in Norman, two suburban locations, a four-story warehouse near downtown and an auto center at Northwest Thirty-Ninth and Pennsylvania Streets. *Ajax Delvecki's collection.*

Della had worked tirelessly through the 1960s. She led Brown's through the civil rights and urban renewal crises and along the way picked up commendations from the Oklahoma Senate and was inducted into the Oklahoma Hall of Fame. Finally, as her health began to fail, she ensured the store's future through astute succession planning. Death came for her on the evening of April 24, 1967, at St. Anthony Hospital. She was eighty-four.

Before a crowded auditorium of mourners at Crown Heights Methodist Church, Bishop W. Angie Smith eulogized Della as a "remarkable character, a gracious leader and a magnetic businesswoman. Almost shy in the public gaze, she was honored by business associates and recognized by all for her great contribution to the social, education, religious and business life of Oklahoma City. Her heart was in downtown Oklahoma City. There was never a thought or expectation of deserting it."

There was a familiar face among the mourners that Wednesday afternoon in April—Clara Luper. In her autobiography, Clara recalled:

> *When she died, I couldn't control my emotions. I went to her funeral and followed the procession to her final resting place. A white executive of the store said, "I'm glad you came."*
>
> *She was my friend. I loved her and I had to come.*

9
"The Trend!"

Because of Della Dunkin Brown's meticulous planning, the John A. Brown Company smoothly transitioned into the next phase of the store's history. Included in her will was a provision for her four top advisors to operate John A. Brown's as a trusteeship. One trustee, Laura Ambrose, who had been vice-president under Della since 1940, became the president of the John A. Brown Company. Joining Ambrose were the company's attorney, Roy C. Lytle; accountant Orba Greenwood; and Kermit Hardwick, onetime store manager of the downtown Brown's and later general manager for the company.

The trustees were instructed to sell the company to a retail chain of national prominence. Della had already come to an agreement with the Sperry & Hutchinson Company of New York to offer them the right of first refusal to purchase the John A. Brown Company. The company's S&H Green Stamps were peaking in popularity as a customer loyalty program in the mid-1960s, and Brown's even featured a redemption shop in the downtown store where customers could redeem books filled with stamps in exchange for merchandise. At the time of Della's death, S&H had been exploring the feasibility of diversifying into direct retail ownership, but they ultimately chose not to exercise their right to purchase Brown's.

Unfortunately, neither witnesses nor records of the trustees' efforts to find a buyer for John A. Brown are extant. There actually were not many prominent national chains for which Brown's would have been a good fit. The largest chains, of course, were of the single-branded type like Sears,

Penney's and Ward's. Federated Department Stores would have been a possible buyer, but the company was already heavily invested in the Sanger-Harris chain in Dallas and Foley's in Houston and didn't see Oklahoma City as a viable market for the chain's plans for the foreseeable future (both brands would have stores in Oklahoma City and Tulsa by the early 1990s). Only a few years before, Federated had pulled out of Oklahoma City when it closed the Halliburton's store on Main Street in 1961.

By 1970, after three years of trusteeship, two serious contenders for Brown's emerged—Dillard's and Dayton-Hudson. In the decade since William T. Dillard purchased Tulsa's Brown-Dunkin from Della Brown and Jane Dunkin, Dillard's Department Stores had been on a solid upward trajectory. Acquiring Brown's would have given Dillard's a hegemony in Oklahoma, as no other stores offered a competitive challenge to Dillard's in terms of the quality and diversity of merchandise offered. The purchase would also give Dillard's a store in every mall in the state's two largest cities and would mean that Dillard's would not have to compete with Brown's in any future mall projects like the planned Crossroads Mall.

To the casual observer, Dillard's made sense as a buyer for Brown's because it offered similar lines of merchandise and they both operated in the same market. Beyond the sales floor, though, the two couldn't have been more different. Dillard's was an aggressive-growth company while Brown's was content to ponderously expand within its home city. William Dillard operated his company by the strict business principles he learned at Columbia University and using the most advanced computer models available for sales and distribution. John A. Brown was led by knowledgeable and experienced executives, but they knew little outside the world of Brown's and continued to operate based on the tenets set forth by the founder over fifty years before. That's not to say that Brown's wasn't a successful company; it was, but the values that made Brown's the greatest store in Oklahoma—the dedication to customer service and the consideration that employees were family—simply would not be a priority under a Dillard's regime.

The other Brown's bidder, Dayton-Hudson Corporation out of Minneapolis, had similarities to both Dillard's and John A. Brown's. The company had begun as Dayton's Department Store in 1902 in downtown Minneapolis and eventually became the greatest store in Minnesota, operating for nearly fifty years as a family store following the philosophies of its founder, George B. Dayton. In the mid-1950s, a third generation of family leadership initiated a period of radical innovation and aggressive growth. It began to purchase regional chains like Lipman's in Portland, Oregon, and it built the first-ever enclosed mall, Southdale Center in suburban Edina, Minnesota, installing its first expansion store there.

Dayton Corporation recognized the growing discount sector in retail (e.g., TG&Y and K-Mart), and in 1962, it refined the concept to start a chain of discount stores in a separate division called Target, though it continued to diversify by creating the B. Dalton Booksellers chain and acquiring regional chains in California, Boston and Philadelphia.

In 1967, Dayton Corporation went public with its initial stock offering about six months after Della Brown's death. Eighteen months later, it purchased the J.L. Hudson Company of Detroit and renamed the company Dayton-Hudson Corporation. Hudson's was similar to Dayton's and Brown's in terms of regional importance, although its flagship store building on Woodward Avenue in Detroit was full of mind-bending superlatives (tallest store in the world, seventy-six elevators and forty-eight escalators, over seven hundred fitting rooms) as the second-largest store in the country behind the Thirty-Fourth Street Macy's in New York.

Though similar to Dillard's in the sense of being a corporation on a course of aggressive growth, Dayton-Hudson shared Brown's customer-centered approach to quality merchandise at value prices, and the company believed strongly in the welfare of their employees—it was the first major company in the retail sector to introduce retirement plans and health insurance for its employees. The Brown's trusteeship was encouraged by two other factors at play with a Dayton-Hudson purchase. One was that the company continued to be committed to large downtown stores. The other was that Brown's had been a family-run operation for fifty years, and the main constituent parts of Dayton-Hudson (Dayton's, Hudson's and Lipman's) were family-run as well. And Dayton-Hudson operated each large acquisition as a separate division, allowing wide latitude in the management of the division and hoping to retain local loyalties and identities in their original markets.

And it was Brown's identity as the state's largest and most popular store that attracted Dayton-Hudson. As it was, Brown's wasn't that large of a chain, with four stores in metro Oklahoma City and none in Tulsa. But as William Dillard had noticed, besides Dillard's, Brown's didn't have any natural competitors in the state. Because they had stores in each city already and a reputation in the Southwest, Dillard's did not need the Brown's identity. And William Dillard wasn't going to pay for it. For Dayton-Hudson, the name meant they could buy in at the top of the wide-open Oklahoma market.

Just months after purchasing the Diamond's chain in Phoenix, Dayton-Hudson outbid "a number of other concerns," including Dillard's, for the

John A. Brown Company. In announcing the sale at a January 20, 1971 press conference, board chairman Bruce B. Dayton told members of the Oklahoma City Chamber of Commerce that his company was "greatly impressed with the strength of the [Oklahoma City] economy and the enlightened way you are planning your future."

Paul Strasbaugh, executive secretary of the chamber, intoned the magnitude of the sale. "This is one of the most significant developments in the retail field in Oklahoma City in two decades. It will further strengthen our redevelopment hopes and plans for the central business district."

In retrospect, it seems as though two different press conferences were taking place simultaneously because a close read of Dayton's comments would not have encouraged such optimism on the part of those interested in Oklahoma City's urban renewal. Dayton made no promises, of course, but he did say that the downtown store was in an "old building" and that he would "look for the location of new stores in areas like Penn Square." He also said that Brown's was strong in offering "quality merchandise and broad assortments" while Dayton-Hudson's strength was in high fashion and that he was excited to see what came of the combination of strengths. Any doubt about the parent company's strength in high fashion would give way to the fact that the only store in the country outside New York to secure an appearance by supermodel Twiggy was Dayton's.

The public reaction to the Brown's sale was swift and heartfelt. A *Daily Oklahoman* columnist wrote, "Most importantly, the downtown Oklahoma City John A. Brown store remained a stabilizing influence during that area's most traumatic years." High school English teacher Lucille Searcy sent a letter to Bruce Dayton that the company used to its advantage:

> *I stood in the kitchen in my robe early this morning, scanning the headlines of the morning paper before I got activated for the day: "Dayton-Hudson Buys John A. Brown Stores."*
>
> *Beyond the glance of my eye, through the door to where our dining table stands, I glimpsed the edge of the big eight-foot braided rug that came from Brown's carpet floor some years ago. On the shelf of the cupboard just behind me was the jar of non-salt baking powder that we buy in the food shop at Brown's. Hanging in the closet is the new dress, not yet worn, bought last week from Brown's Town and Country Shop. Right now, as I type, I can see the candy-striped sheet on my bed, bought at Brown's, and three hat-boxes of my last pretty hats (I am an old lady and wear lots of hats) from Brown's Millinery. The black pumps on my feet right now come from Brown's.*

> *When Mrs. John A. Brown died, we said, "There it goes. When they do away with Brown's, we stop shopping in Oklahoma City. We almost never go out to one of the shopping centers. We can remember the old, old days when we went up to the city on the interurban (We called it "the galloping goose") and trudged through the Christmas snow to look in Brown's fantastic windows. Brown's was the center of Main Street.*
>
> *Don't change it too much yet, for awhile. It seems to have almost everything that the average person needs. Don't let it turn into a dime-store clutter effect—as I remember some of my childhood fairyland stores changing in St. Louis. We have carried a charge account there at Brown's for years. We are not your biggest buyers, but there are lots of little people like us. We like Brown's and don't want to lose it.*
>
> *Lucile Searcy*
> *Jean Sugden*

The company reprinted the letter in the *Oklahoma Journal* the following week and replied:

> *Lots of people feel like you do. Many letters and calls have told us so...but, let us tell you about Dayton-Hudson: Founded in 1902, it is headed today by the two grandsons. It, too, is a family store and intends to keep Brown's exactly the same way. Our name will not change. Our integrity will not change, and the store will continue to lead Oklahoma forward in continuing community progress.*
>
> *May we also tell you that Dayton-Hudson is very glad to have joined this family. So, Lucile Searcy, rest assured, you'll approve of everything that happens in the future at John A. Brown Company.*

Within a month, Dayton-Hudson appointed a new president for Brown's. He was James Sherburne, a brash Oregonian who had been vice-president and general manager of Phoenix's Diamond's Department Store, which was acquired by Dayton-Hudson in early 1968. In replacing the seventy-nine-year-old Laura Ambrose as president, Sherburne gave praise saying, "Under her leadership the company achieved record sales and expanded its reputation for quality and service." Ambrose was excited, too, saying that the thirty-seven-year-old Sherburne was "a young, aggressive merchant who will lead Brown's...to undertake the expansion we have long envisioned for the company."

Sherburne wasted no time in setting out on the expansion plan. Indeed, the first move had actually been made in November 1970, when Dayton-Hudson purchased the lease of the Vandever's Department Store in Tulsa's upscale outdoor mall, Utica Square, with the intent to install a seventy-thousand-square-foot Diamond's store there. With the addition of Brown's to the Dayton-Hudson fold, the company simply converted it to a John A. Brown before the Diamond's store ever opened.

In Oklahoma City, Sherburne spent $500,000 to modernize the downtown and Capitol Hill Brown's stores in November 1971. Legendary city interior designer John Bullard removed the old fluorescent strip lighting, walls and dividers to create an open space he said was inspired by Oklahoma's sweeping prairies. Where the old Brown's had merchandise in cases and shelves lining the walls, Bullard placed them in open areas on tables and display furniture, which he lined with sleek chrome trim to enhance the lighting effects. The old building still had some nooks and crannies, and Bullard filled them with mini boutiques like one might find in a bazaar or European village. One was called "Outta Sight" and featured strange and unusual merchandise, and there was a candle shop and an antique shop, among others. The new management also added new services to the wide variety that Brown's already offered, including a flower shop and a bookstore. When Sherburne noticed that Oklahoma City's affluent shoppers made trips to Texas to buy their luxury goods—especially after the demise of Kerr's—Brown's also began offering top-level merchandise with the expressed intent of keeping local customers from traveling to Neiman-Marcus in Dallas.

Despite the upgrade, the future of the downtown store was still cloudy. With Urban Renewal Project 1-B, which included the Galleria retail complex, still at least five years away in 1971, Brown's new leadership mulled over the future of Brown's in the downtown area. Merchandise manager Sherm Swenson pondered, "The only question right now is do we build a new downtown store or would we be better off to spend more money on this charming old building which is expensive and unique. It's the old-fashionedness of the downtown store that makes it so adorable." A month later, downtown officials got their first hint of the answer when Brown's announced they would be an anchor in the new Crossroads Mall planned for 1974.

In all, Sherburne was impressed with his new home. "This is the most full-service department store I have ever seen," he said. "But some of the departments were merely in existence and not offering the best service to the customer." It's so familiar to modern shoppers as to seem rather

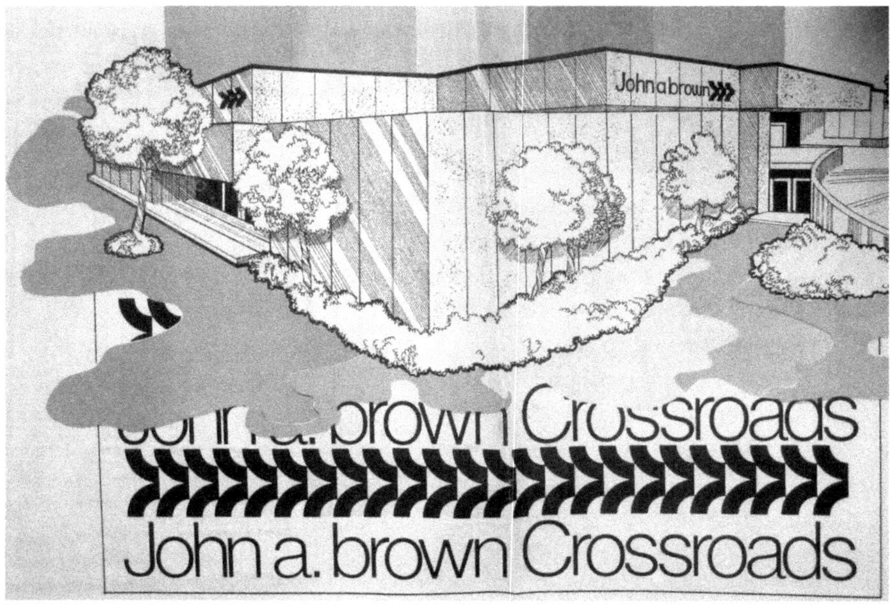

The opening of the Crossroads Mall store in February 1974 signaled a shift in focus from a one-stop shop to a fashion hub. *Ajax Delvecki's collection.*

obvious, but an immediate change Dayton-Hudson made was to reorganize the departments by purpose rather than by classification. For example, it created a Bath Shop where one could find towels, bathroom accessories and bathmats in one place rather than expecting the shopper to visit the towel department, home accessory department and the rug department.

Brown's other stores in Penn Square and Capitol Hill were also reorganized along the lines downtown had been, though the most notable change occurred at the College Shop in Norman. "It isn't really a College Shop at all," Sherburne said, adding that it had evolved to serve the needs of permanent Norman residents as much or more than university students. Despite the addition of another "Outta Sight" shop, Norman was reorganized to reflect the needs of the wider community.

Another big change was in the return policy—under Dayton-Hudson, Brown's would take anything back for a refund. No receipt, no problem. They even took back merchandise that wasn't purchased at Brown's. They also ramped up the advertising budget. Despite, or because of, its size and importance, the old Brown's did not place a lot of stake in advertising, usually only three to five half-page ads a week. The new advertising campaign was called "Explore the World of Brown's" and was focused on simply getting people into the stores as much as promoting merchandise. "We want to show them that we are carrying out our own urban renewal program," Sherburne said.

Meanwhile, in October 1972, about eighteen months after Dayton-Hudson acquired Brown's, Sherburne was asked about recent delays in the progress of Project 1-B, specifically the obstacles in acquiring the real estate on which a new downtown store could be built. He lamented that it seemed further away than ever and that the turn of events was "disappointing" because the company wanted a new downtown space. He was less concerned about the new property than the overall abandonment of downtown. "We've noticed some drop [in sales] because of the moves of nearby businesses," he said. "Businesses do better together."

The final piece of John A. Brown's rejuvenated image came with a new company logo in the autumn of 1973. The corporate marketing department devised the symbol, consisting of three stylized chevrons in a forward-leaning position, and the company held a contest to determine a name for the symbol. Brown's received thousands of entries, which a panel of judges narrowed to eleven possibilities: Key to Quality, Pointing with Pride, Trendtrack, Wings of the Future, Dependagram, Ultra-Progression, the Shooting Star, Forward Flare, Service by Design, Rising to New Heights and, the winner, Friendagon. The $300 winning entry was sent in by Vietnam veteran and Southwestern Oklahoma State College student John F. Leebron. Executives said they selected it because "besides quality fashion and value, you have a friend in John A. Brown."

As the grand opening of the huge Crossroads Mall neared in early 1974, word finally came about the future of the downtown store—sort of. In February, James Sherburne announced that Dayton-Hudson executives advised him that both the downtown and Capitol Hill stores would close in July. The closings were timed to coincide with the opening of the 150,000-square-foot Brown's store at Crossroads (it opened six months after the mall opened). The ninety-seven-acre Crossroads was a truly regional mall, accommodating fifty thousand shoppers per day, he explained, and its service area easily encompassed that of the Capitol Hill store and would help alleviate the temporary loss of the downtown store. Sherburne also laid out the next few years for John A. Brown's. After the opening of the Crossroads store in August 1974, next up would be a new Quail Springs Mall and a store at Tulsa's Woodland Hills Mall in 1976. Then a return to downtown was planned for the Galleria in 1977.

One final look at the historic Main Street location, 1975. *Kenyon Morgan Collection, RetroMetroOKC.*

With the candidness typical of the open management style of the Dayton-Hudson Brown's, the employee newsletter following Sherburne's announcement printed an item called "Overheard Comments":

> *The recent announcement by our store president Jim Sherburne, foretelling the closing of the Capitol Hill and Downtown stores was comparable to an historic event. Several overheard comments from employees were:*
> *"We are a landmark and an institution. I always thought the Downtown store would remain."*
> *"It's just sad."*
> *"Now there will be no more rumors."*
> *"I'm relieved that it's out it in the open."*
> *"Having previously read about the Galleria, you couldn't help but read between the lines."*
> *"I'm glad we're getting a new building. Every time they take a board out I'm always afraid it'll be the wrong one and the store will completely collapse!"*

Going forward, John A Brown's was to implement what Sherburne called "environmental shopping," which was a further refinement of reorganization they did at downtown. Merchandisers identified five shopping environments (men's, women's, children's, home and leisure), and each item was grouped into one of the environments, or zones. So while the Crossroads store was readied for opening, the Penn Square store received a complete overhaul to bring both stores in line with environmental shopping.

The closing of the downtown store was slated for Saturday, July 20, 1974. Beginning on the fourteenth, the "Downtown Sale of Sales" was advertised, offering 60 to 90 percent off all merchandise in the downtown store only. Media coverage of those last days was not as heavy as one might have expected for a fifty-nine-year-old store, but the one small feature penned by the *Daily Oklahoman*'s Linda Welch adequately summed up the history and mystique of this Oklahoma City institution. Welch presented downtown employee Aliece Gram as the centerpiece for her eulogy of downtown Brown's. Gram began her career at the age of twenty-one when she applied to Rorabaugh-Brown's the week after it changed from Brock's in 1915. "Mr. Brown hired me," she said. "We didn't have a personnel manager then." Gram had worked for Brown's for fifty-nine years, forty-six of them in the silver department. She was the embodiment of what Brown's meant to city shoppers, and she credited the customers for keeping her working long after retirement age. "I've been with some of the customers so long; I love them," she said. "When they [regular customers] don't come in I call them and see why they don't come in. When I find something in the store that I think a particular customer would like, I call them and tell them about it." Even so, Gram wasn't quitting. She intended on giving the Penn Square store a try even though she wasn't sure at the time how she would get to work. She didn't drive, and the bus dropped her right in front of the downtown store. Aliece worked two more years at Penn Square and retired after sixty-one years at Brown's. She died in 1987 at the age of ninety-three.

Reporter Tom McCarthy covered the downtown store's last day, which he said, "had more the feeling of an Irish wake than a funeral." He described "swarms of women shoppers chatting contentedly" as they ransacked piles of remaindered merchandise while "veteran employees [were] still standing as noble sentinels behind their display cases, even though the display cases were empty." In all, he said it was "a high-spirited and decadent scene." Finally, at 5:30 p.m., the doors were locked, and the original John A. Brown's store closed for the last time. McCarthy signed off saying, "John A. Brown passed from revered history into the bleak present of downtown Oklahoma City."

Downtown store manager R.H. Carr hangs the final "Closed" sign, signaling the end of fifty-nine years as a major downtown attraction, July 20, 1974. *Photo by Cliff Traverse; Oklahoma Historical Society, the Gateway to Oklahoma History.*

The following week was a busy one for John A. Brown's. As Dayton-Hudson president Kenneth N. Dayton planned a visit to Oklahoma City to formally open the new Crossroads Mall and the remodeled Penn Square stores, store personnel planned a number of celebrations—open house receptions, fashion shows, big-band concerts and a champagne reception with ballroom dancing at Crossroads, as well as a speaking engagement for Dayton before the Oklahoma City Chamber of Commerce on "the future of John A. Brown."

During a lunchtime address at the chamber's Friday Forum, Dayton gave an unexpected answer to the question of Brown's future. He began by expressing Brown's commitment to the state and pointed to the two major mall expansions that were a couple years off, as well as Target's growth in Tulsa and Oklahoma City. Dayton also gave a long discussion on why retail stores locate where they do and outlined the requirements retailers must meet before deciding to remain in a central city location. "If suburban shopping centers are popular because they are easy to reach, the downtown must become easier to reach. If shopping centers offer an exciting atmosphere, the downtown must offer its own unique brand of excitement. But shopping centers have learned what downtown executives have always known—business goes where there is the most business."

He went on to extol the virtues of public mass transit and limiting urban sprawl and directed chamber members to consider the new urban resident in 1970s America—one who has a "new questioning and searching for what the term 'quality of life' means." What he did not do was commit Brown's to the Galleria project. Still, in a *Daily Oklahoman* editorial the next day, chamber president Ed Cook expressed his encouragement at Dayton's speech and felt certain that Brown's would be among the first to return to the downtown area when the Galleria was completed. "The new tunnels, already glamorous and soon to be featuring new concourse level shops, restaurants and clubs," the editorial said, "represent the faith of many in the central city as a viable concept." As the anonymous Brown's employee remarked in the newsletter, "You couldn't help but read between the lines."

As soon as Capitol Hill closed, Brown's executives remodeled the building into a rather spacious corporate headquarters. And John A. Brown's closed

The 150,000-square-foot store at Crossroads opened on August 5, 1974, to great fanfare. *Kenyon Morgan Collection, RetroMetroOKC.*

out a busy 1974 with an auction of all the contents of the downtown Brown's store that could not be used at Crossroads. The facility manager at the store lamented that it took so long to clear out the old hulk of a building because maintenance staff kept uncovering stashes of merchandise in hidden caches all over the store. Beyond the expected things like display cases and shelving, the auction also included two new pre-1932 pull chain toilets, an unused wood slat park bench, and a fancy boudoir screen.

Under James Sherburne, Brown's continued to expand steadily throughout the 1970s. Although slowed a bit by a national retail slump from 1973 to 1975, planning continued for two regional malls in Tulsa and another in Oklahoma City. In 1976, Dayton-Hudson and Sears cooperatively built Tulsa's Woodland Hills Mall regional shopping center—Sears bought the 155-acre site and Dayton-Hudson built the two-story mall building at East Seventy-First Street and South Memorial Drive. Sherburne was keen for that store to come online because it was inefficient to operate the small Utica Square store as the only store in Tulsa. Company officials also hoped for a mall on the east side of Tulsa, too, and it's unclear whether this meant the abortive Eastland Mall, conceived in 1969 but delayed in opening until 1986.

Dayton-Hudson was also a developing partner in Quail Springs Mall at Memorial and Pennsylvania. On this venture, JCPenney was the co-developer, and Sears and Dillard's rounded out the other anchor stores.

Once considered an upscale shopping destination, Capitol Hill felt the pinch of the retail exodus to shopping malls, 1977. *Photo by Doug Hoke; Oklahoma Historical Society, the Gateway to Oklahoma History.*

Newly appointed division president James Miller outside the Quail Springs store in 1982. His optimism was short-lived. After the John A. Brown name was retired, Penn Square became Dillard's. Crossroads and Quail Springs became Sanger-Harris, Foley's and finally Macy's, 1982. *Photo by Roger Klock; Oklahoma Historical Society, the Gateway to Oklahoma History.*

Quail Springs had a rocky development path like Eastland, though much less severe. Planning began in 1972 when a development group led by W.P. "Bill" Atkinson purchased two large tracts of empty land bound by May, Penn, Northwest 150th and Northwest 122nd. The initial goal was a "dream city" of residential and commercial development, and the land for the mall was sold to co-op development company DayJay Associates. At ninety-five acres and 1.2 million square feet of space, it was substantially smaller than Crossroads Mall, though it was expected to serve the entirety of the northern and western periphery of the metro area and the surrounding counties. The opening was planned for 1977, but a series of delays pushed it back to spring and then autumn of 1980.

In March 1980, six months before the Quail Springs store was set to open, James Sherburne resigned as president of the John A. Brown Company to head the Fort Worth division of Dillard's. At Brown's, Sherburne was overseer for six stores, but for Dillard's, he shepherded twenty stores in six states. Casual observers often dismiss Sherburne and, indeed, the entire

Dayton-Hudson era as somehow responsible for the demise of Brown's or, at the very least, as an example of what happens to local institutions when national corporations devour them. Such opinions are unfounded and unfair in this case, though. To begin with, Dayton-Hudson allowed Brown's to operate as a completely autonomous entity that received all the benefits of corporate resources but none of the micromanagement. Thus, it would be fair to say that although Dayton-Hudson and Sherburne were not native to Oklahoma, John A. Brown's was still a local store.

Indeed, James Sherburne had many similarities with Brown's company founder, Bert Brown. He was honest and open with his employees and was possessed of a genuinely friendly demeanor. He was also a dynamic leader, and employees were energized by the culture of change and modernization in the stores. Sherburne also shared Bert's acumen at assessing financial conditions and, like Brown, was frequently sought by local news for opinion on all manner of business matters from the retail sector to the energy crisis.

Sherburne had an acute instinct for evaluating the Oklahoma retail sector. He recognized early on that city shoppers were generally more traditional and conservative, in terms of both fashion risk and willingness to spend money, than other markets Dayton-Hudson served. Consequently, he took a more aggressive course in advertising and promotion than other stores in the Dayton-Hudson fold, essentially educating Oklahoma consumers on what to wear and when to buy it. To that end, he created two concepts for his employees—"first in, first out" and "clarity of offer." He knew that fashion followers liked newness, and he knew that Oklahoma's conservative shoppers wouldn't buy something at full price one month when they knew they could get it for half the next month. So he pressed his buyers and merchandisers to be the first in to a particular season and the first out. Customers often found bathing suits for sale in January and unavailable by July or winter coats hanging on racks in the summer and gone by the end of autumn. The "clarity of offer" concept simply meant that store personnel should bring together the most popular and bestselling styles and products and place them in conspicuous places to make them easy for shoppers to find. The result was a reorganization of the stores in the early '70s. This was a departure from a downtown Brown's store that was laid out in such a way as to encourage customers to get lost and wander through the store.

Finally, like Bert Brown, Sherburne was also an active member in the city's cultural and charitable life. Dayton-Hudson already had a policy of returning 5 percent of its profits back to the communities it served (and still does as Target Corporation), but Sherburne and his wife, Marilyn, went

With the popularity of the mall locations, Dayton-Hudson was able to target its ideal market: upscale, fashion conscious customers, 1976. *Photo by Bob Albright; Oklahoma Historical Society, the Gateway to Oklahoma History.*

beyond corporate obligations and gave generously of their time by working as organizers and fundraisers for many local arts and charity organizations.

In May 1980, Sherburne formally transferred the reins of John A. Brown Company over to new president Thomas G. Payne, who came to Oklahoma City from Detroit, where he was vice-president of Brown's corporate sister store, Hudson's. Payne would work out a two-year tenure as Brown's president before returning to Hudson's in 1982 to become president of that eighteen-store chain. Though the company did not expand under his watch, he oversaw the renovation of all Brown's stores to bring them up to par with the new Quail Springs store, including yet another renovation of the Penn Square store as the mall converted from an open-air to an indoor mall. Under Payne, John A. Brown's sales doubled from $47 million to $95 million, though much of that was due to the addition of the Quail Springs store in October 1980.

Employee Sarah Grilley accidentally began a career as Brown's first-ever gift wrapper. She retired after fifty years of service in 1984. *Photo by Steve Gooch; Oklahoma Historical Society, the Gateway to Oklahoma History.*

In early August 1982, just weeks after the failure of Penn Square Bank, Tom Payne was succeeded by Jim Miller, a thirty-something graduate of Dayton-Hudson's executive training program. He'd worked his way through the ranks as manager, buyer and merchandiser and, in 1980, followed Payne to Brown's as vice-president. Miller was the last president of John A. Brown Company, as the company was sold to Dillard's a year and a half after he took charge.

At the time of the sale to Dillard's in mid-1984, news accounts pointed to lackluster sales caused by the Penn Square Bank crash and the oil glut, which caused a collapse in crude oil prices. Indeed, the last corporate earnings report for Dayton-Hudson indicated Brown's profit was down 32 percent from 1983. The stores were

This final issue of the company newsletter showcased the many facets of the downtown location, with a quick view of the historical Capitol Hill and Norman locations. *Ajax Delvecki's collection.*

still profitable but at a much lower level. This was compelling evidence that Brown's was slipping, but how much of it was to be blamed on the economy is unknown. The fact is that Dayton-Hudson had begun a shift from traditional department stores to discount stores in the late 1970s when their Target

The downtown store was vacant for two years before demolition began in July 1976. Today, the space is part of the Devon Energy complex. *Photo by Don Tullous; Oklahoma Historical Society, the Gateway to Oklahoma History.*

stores had become their most profitable division (the corporation renamed itself Target Corporation in 2000). The corporation bought California discount chain Mervyn's in 1978, and in 1980, it sold off the more traditional Lipman's stores to Marshall Field's. It also closed some Hudson's stores (including the downtown Detroit store) in 1983. In retrospect, it seems unloading Diamond's and Brown's was as much the corporate plan as it was economic necessity.

Regardless of the reason for its demise, the John A. Brown Company ceased to exist on September 24, 1984, when the sale to Dillard's was finalized—exactly sixty-nine years to the day after A.O. Rorabaugh and Bert Brown took over Brock's.

Part II

KERR'S

10

"There Can Be No Dissatisfaction Here!"

In many ways, the history of Kerr's Department Store parallels that of John A. Brown's. The two stores had similar origins as colonizers from Kansas, began as family operations, were founded about the same time and, of course, eventually operated on the same street in the same city. They were each also strongly influenced by their founders' visions, however divergent those might have been. Where Bert Brown was an effusively extroverted person who viewed the customer as king, George Kerr was more introverted and was more employee-focused, taking the stance that a happy, well-paid employee made for happy customers. Ultimately, both philosophies proved successful in their own right.

If George Kerr's ideas about healthy, happy employees seem anachronistic to the era of union busting and the sixty-hour work week, they were fairly advanced for the early twentieth century, though hardly unique. Kerr himself had been a benefactor of similar ideas as a young employee at two of the most prominent department stores of the late 1800s.

George Gabriel Kerr was born on a farm in 1863 outside the village of Paisley, Ontario, Canada, a mill town just inland from Lake Huron. Many young men bored of tedious farm chores on Huron's shores looked to the merchant marines for escape, but Gabriel, as he was known to those close to him, traveled the 120 miles southeast to Toronto. The city was still the second city of Canada in the 1880s, more Chicago than New York, but it had plenty of bustle. And Kerr wanted to be part of it. He quickly found a position in Eaton's Department Store as a sales clerk, and though he

A merchant and philanthropist, George G. Kerr died before he could see his store go from a simply dry goods establishment to being referred to as the "Neiman-Marcus of Oklahoma." *From* The Story of Oklahoma City, Oklahoma, *vol. 2, 1922.*

wasn't formally an apprentice, he learned a great deal that would make him successful later in his career. Eaton's was already "Canada's Greatest Store" by then, occupying sixty acres of downtown Toronto, and founder Timothy Eaton pioneered things like single cash prices for goods (in the era when bartering and bargaining were the norm) and cash refunds for merchandise, no questions asked. Indeed, the company slogan, "Goods Satisfactory or Money Refunded," was later adapted to fit Kerr's.

George Kerr also took many of Timothy Eaton's feelings about his employees to heart. Eaton had struggled as a laborer in Northern Ireland as a youth, and he was determined that his employees would not lead lives of privation for themselves and their families. He shortened working hours (twelve hours was the common workday), created paid holidays and even pioneered a rudimentary health plan for his seventeen thousand employees. A voracious compiler and consumer of statistics generated by his huge retail enterprise, Eaton also realized the store sold more merchandise when his employees were happier, healthier and better paid.

After a few years at Eaton's, Kerr moved on to the Mandel Brothers store in Chicago. Mandel Brothers was a huge store (at one time considered the largest department store outside New York) at the corner of Madison and State Streets in the Loop. It was there that Kerr learned about upscale merchandising, as Mandel Brothers bought goods not only from the New York markets but also from Europe's finest.

Kerr spent a year or so in Chicago before landing in Kansas, learning more about the dry goods trade for a couple more years before moving to Oklahoma City in 1897. During his first tenure in the city, he worked in the Clay-Widemeyer Company's Lion Store. This was amid a period of economic downturn in Oklahoma City, and after only a few months, he took an opportunity to partner with W.H. Brennand in a store in Big Spring, Texas. There he met and wed Jessie Smith in 1900. Over the six years since leaving Oklahoma City in 1897, Kerr partnered in stores in Big Spring and Corsicana, Texas, and another in California. In December 1903, he returned to Oklahoma City and worked as a floor manager for Mellon's, but he was quickly wooed away to manage the Kennedy Brothers Dry Goods Company store at 226 West Main Street near the southeast corner of Main and Harvey. Richard and William Kennedy had a modest string of stores based in Enid, Oklahoma, with stores in Kingfisher and Oklahoma City. They opened a small storefront at 140 West Main Street in 1901 and brought Kerr in to manage when they expanded into the larger building down the street.

This was a time of intense competition among a number of small dry goods stores like Mellon's, Brock's, Sturm's, May Brothers and others. Full-scale department stores were not long in coming, and Kennedy Brothers did well enough in Oklahoma City. In 1907, a consortium made up of Charles Gideon Bulkley, a retailer in Salina, Kansas; Bulkley's son, Willard Spencer Bulkley, a banker and retailer in Pawnee, Oklahoma; Bulkley's son-in-law, Frederick O. Lutz, a retailer in Guthrie; and Kerr bought out the Kennedy brothers' interest and reopened as Kerr Dry Goods Company. Like Bert Brown, George Kerr was given wide latitude in running the store.

As one would expect of a man who had spent so much time under the tutelage of others, George Kerr bolted from the gate when the time came to operate his own place. His employees were his most valuable asset, he reasoned, and he instituted a paid half holiday for them every Thursday afternoon, closing the store at 1:00 p.m. on those days. When quizzed about it later, he said his sales were better the rest of the week and easily made up for the lost half day. Kerr also hosted large banquets for his staff. After $5,000 was expended on an affair at the Huckins Hotel in 1910, it drew the notice of the business desk at the *Oklahoman*. They could find no other company in the Southwest and certainly not in Oklahoma City that cared as much for the welfare of its employees. The newspaper reasoned that "whatever the monetary loss [the company] suffered, it was overwhelmed by the spirit of loyalty and good feeling shown on every side." An employee representative said the company would make up the lost money "by efficient and loyal service which the employees will show in return. I feel sure [the employee] better able to do his or her work intelligently and, best of all, with an understanding that he or she is appreciated." In the coming years, Kerr also created a rudimentary health insurance plan and hired a matron to look after the well-being of the young, unmarried salesgirls.

Far from simple pampering, the results of Kerr's investment in his employees were not long in coming. After a year and a few months, the company's sales were brisk, and the company outgrew its small storefront and single floor of sales space. Oklahoma City was in the midst of an economic boom, and Kerr's became the store of choice for the city's rising middle class. Kerr's buyers scoured the world for premium merchandise, and the sales staff lavished attention on these shoppers. One official was quoted in an article about the attention women received in the store, "The men? We don't care much about the men, although we're glad to have them here to act as gallant escorts."

In early 1909, Kerr's bore the cost of remodeling the four-story building it rented into a retail palace. The first floor offered general dry goods and was finished in rich mahogany. The men's and women's departments on the second floor were outfitted with lush carpeting and Mission furniture. The principal attraction was the peacefully inviting Japanese room, which allowed shoppers to rest, sip tea and relax. Subsequent floors were less elegant in oak trim, and children's goods, fabrics and store offices could be found on those floors. A sleek elevator carried shoppers between floors.

Advertising was also a pillar in the Kerr's business plan. While Rorabaugh-Brown's advertised only a few days of the week with smaller ads, Kerr's took out half-page ads every day of the week. These ads were a fixture on the back page of the *Oklahoman*—easily found by flipping the morning paper over each day. The ads were created by a professional staff and were accompanied by elegant fashion illustrations.

Despite a series of personal tragedies, Kerr's prospered throughout the World War I era. Kerr's partner F.O. Lutz suffered from cancer and had been in Europe throughout most of 1914 seeking advanced treatment. Feeling he might be in his final days and without concern for the German U-boats patrolling the Atlantic, he boarded a ship hoping to spend his last Christmas in Oklahoma. He died at sea on Christmas Day.

In August 1915, Kerr's had outgrown its four-story building and secured a ten-year lease on the six-story Security Building from W.T. Hales. The building was adjacent to the original store (which it continued to occupy) to the west and gave the store a 100-foot storefront on Main Street and 150 feet on Harvey for 77,000 square feet total. Kerr heralded the move as a major upgrade that would allow an expansion into new lines of merchandise, making Kerr's a full department store. Characteristic of George Kerr, he insisted on staff lounges for all employees in the new space "It has always been my idea that…the sales force should be taken care of first," he told newspapers. "And now that this situation has arisen I am going to see that every provision for their comfort and welfare is made." The new store opened in February 1916.

In January 1919, the store was thrown into mourning when the store's twenty-nine-year-old advertising whiz kid, Lucien Segar, succumbed to the Spanish influenza epidemic. A few weeks later, news came from the East Coast that George Kerr was gravely ill there. In New York on a buying trip, he accidentally stepped on a space heater in his hotel room, resulting in severe burns on his foot. He did not consider it a serious injury; however, he was already in poor health from a kidney ailment (commonly called Bright's

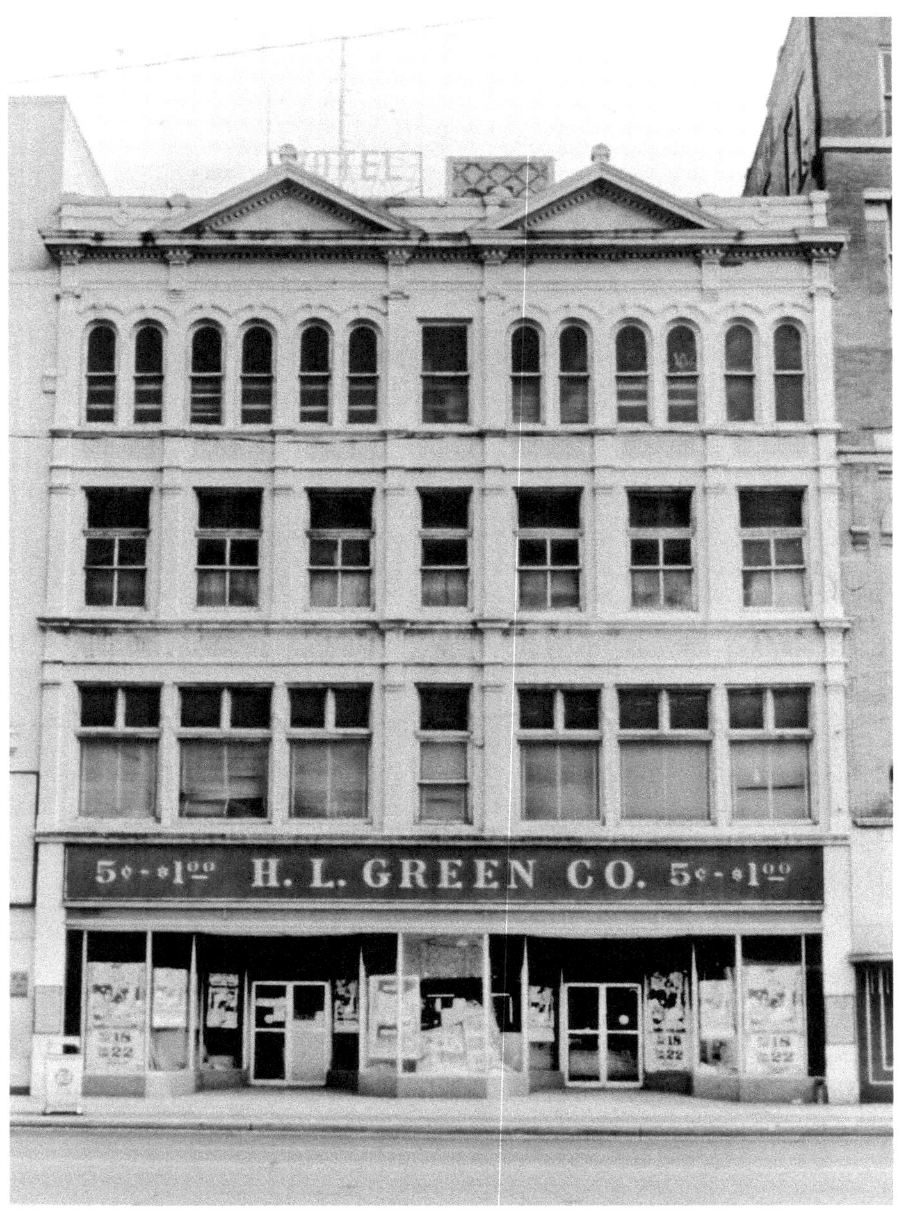

The original Kennedy Brothers/Kerr's store later became an H.L. Green branch and remained a fixture of Oklahoma City's "Dime Store Row" until the 1970s. *Kenyon Morgan Collection, RetroMetroOKC.*

disease then), and the burn worsened into blood poisoning. His wife, Jessie, and his partner W.S. Bulkley rushed to his bedside in a New Jersey hospital. He died on March 4, 1919.

When employees were informed that the store was closing out of respect for the passing of Kerr, a discernible pall was cast about the place. Some employees stood motionless at their stations while others gathered in small groups in the aisles. No one was quite sure whether to believe the news, nor did they know where to go from there. Reportedly, all 260 were present at the funeral service at First Presbyterian Church. Besides the expected accolades great men receive at their funerals from bishops and chamber of commerce presidents, George Kerr received the following particularly poignant eulogy from his closest friend, M.D. Scott of Scott-Halliburton Department Store:

> *To know him was to love him. His acquaintance was one of those privileges that men are sometimes permitted to enjoy. He was genial, affable, fair, honest, philanthropic. Although he was a competitor, he was one of those rare people who could be a competitor and a friend at the same time. My intimate, personal friend has passed out into the great unknown, but the works he performed will live on, forever and a day.*

II

"The Whole Town's Talking"

George Kerr's partner Willard Spencer Bulkley assumed control of the store after the George's passing. Born in Chicago in 1872, Bulkley grew up in Kansas and participated in the family store in Salina, Kansas, with his brother, Fred, and father, Charles. Bulkley was primarily a banker and largely occupied himself with running the Local Building and Loan Association (later Local Federal) and even served as director of the Kansas City Federal Reserve Bank in the 1920s. Kerr built the store on a solid foundation, though, and Bulkley generally continued his policies despite marrying them to an expansion plan. Bulkley espoused what he called the Kerr Ideal.—"To build a business that will never know completion, but will advance continually to meet the advancing conditions of our city."

The first move Bulkley made toward the Kerr Ideal was unusual for Oklahoma City retail. He purchased the lots at 312, 314, 316 and 318 West Main Street and constructed a $750,000 eight-story building on the site in 1925. Unlike Brown's (with its seven landlords) and other major stores like Sears and Penney's in later years, Kerr's was the sole owner of its own building on Main Street. When the store—dubbed Greater Kerr's—opened in September, several other Main Street stores devoted ad space in the *Daily Oklahoman* congratulating Kerr's on the sleek and modern building that offered three acres of sales space. Most of the ads were typical platitudes, but Halliburton's ad featured a photo of the Kerr's building as it appeared from Halliburton's front door. The text below read in part, "It is a pleasure to reflect that we again are neighbors and pleasant

Kerr's new location was built in 1925 and was situated between Brown's and Halliburton's. *Oklahoma Mattress Company Collection, RetroMetroOKC.*

memories carry us back a few years when we were located 'just across the street' at Main and Harvey. So, we welcome you, not as a stranger, but as a familiar face in new surroundings. And let us, as 'two old settlers,' clasp hands across the way." John A. Brown's was the only notable store without a congratulatory ad for Kerr's.

The next steps in achieving the Kerr Ideal came with the opening of the Norman store at Boyd and Asp in 1936 and the Uptown store in 1937. Throughout the 1920s and 1930s, Kerr's had been solidifying its place as the leader in higher-quality merchandise in Oklahoma City. The move to Norman made sense for the company because the college was still largely attended by the upper strata of society. Kerr's Campus Shop was all the rage in Norman. Bulkley fostered a relationship with the campus by creating a series of proto-internships with the University of Oklahoma Advertising Club in which students could design ads and dress windows for the store. Kerr's also hired a cadre of students from various sororities to wear Kerr's clothing on campus as sort of walking advertisements.

Above: The two-story Norman location at 223 West Boyd Street operated from 1936 to 1954. Geared toward the college crowd, it sold mostly young men's and women's clothing. *Courtesy of Jay Hughes.*

Right: Kerr's was the first downtown department store to expand out of Main Street. This 1942 ad showcased the Norman location at Boyd and Asp Streets. *The University of Oklahoma,* Sooner Yearbook.

In 1937, true to the Kerr Ideal "to meet the advancing conditions of our city," Bulkley opened Kerr's Uptown at Northwest Twenty-Fourth and Walker Streets. Strategically positioned between neighborhoods in Kerr's target demographic—the Paseo, Mesta Park, Crown Heights and Heritage Hills (as it's known today)—the new store had a glamorously sleek Art Deco façade. Announcements for the new store read:

> *Constantly abreast of the new...the modern...and in keeping with the present trend in merchandising to simplify your shopping problem...we give you Kerr's Uptown...literally a "chip off the old block," bringing "Main Street" out to your very doorstep and eliminating hereafter the greater preparation and extra time required for extra trips to the downtown shopping district. Today a twenty-nine year old Kerr's with new ideas...a business timed to the needs of tomorrow...an organization pervaded by an unceasing and increasing zeal for improvement sets the pace in a modern, fast-growing metropolis.*

Kerr's Uptown opened in 1937. It was always held at a distance and remained positioned an upscale store until it's last day on May 28, 1965, shortly after the opening of Shepherd Mall. *Courtesy of the family of Edward Eason.*

Kerr's Uptown's interior, early 1960s. *Courtesy of the family of Edward Eason.*

Kerr's had indeed emerged as a dynamic and fast-moving company and performed quite well during the Depression era. Unfortunately, W.S. Bulkley was not to enjoy his success for too long. In April 1940, he succumbed to pneumonia, roughly six weeks after Bert Brown died unexpectedly.

To replace Bulkley as president of the company, Henry N. Wyzanski was brought in from the outside. Wyzanski was a thirty-eight-year-old Boston native who had quickly risen to the position as merchandise manager for the Mandel Brothers stores in Chicago—the same store where George Kerr honed his skills.

Wyzanski perpetuated the policies of his predecessors. Like Kerr, he continued the half holidays and employee picnics and banquets for his staff. And in one comical episode during World War II, he was able to use connections to secure some impossibly scarce nylons. The shipment of one thousand pairs allowed each of his five hundred employees to buy two pairs each. When the public heard about it, there was a near riot in the streets, but Wyzanski told the *Daily Oklahoman* that one thousand pairs would be just a drop in the bucket in terms of the overall shortage if they were sold to the public, but it would bring immeasurable goodwill to his employees.

Wyzanski, and his wife, Glenn, maintained Kerr's place as the frontrunner in fashion and style in Oklahoma City throughout the 1940s, as Kerr's top-label clothing was featured at most events on the social calendar and innovations made the store attractive to the nouveau riche. Nothing secured that notion more than the creation of Kerr's Mirror Room, which featured the highest fashion from noted couturiers from around the world. At one time, the Mirror Room was the only shop outside Beverly Hills to offer dresses by Irene, the designer for Hollywood's most glamorous like Ginger Rogers, Lana Turner and Ingrid Bergman, among many others.

In 1943, the store applied to the Federal Aviation Administration for permission to construct a helipad atop its eight-story structure. Plans were to deliver Kerr's merchandise by helicopter to any town in Oklahoma with a population of five thousand or more. An air taxi service was also planned that would ferry shoppers from the civil airport in Bethany to Kerr's for shopping junkets.

Under Henry and Glenn Wyzanski, Kerr's became a nationally known store. The Mirror Room, shown here, solidified the store's glamorous reputation. *Courtesy of the family of Edward Eason.*

Under Wyzanski's energetic leadership, sales quadrupled in just a few years. Beginning in 1944, a series of upgrades to the downtown store exemplified the Kerr's Ideal. Legendary interior designer Dorothy Draper was brought in to redesign the third floor women's and junior's department, culminating in a visit from the illustrious Draper, now regarded as the "stylemaker" of the 1940s, to the delight of Kerr's customers. In 1947, a phased $400,000 expansion began with the acquisition of the Patterson Building, a four-story building to the west. The storefront was extended to 141 feet on Main Street, and air conditioning was installed throughout. The first floor of the new space featured an elaborate $150,000 shoe salon. The décor was divided into three motifs: an outdoor resort motif for casual shoes, an elegant oval room in the center with circular benches covered in exclusive aluminum fabric that showed the best brands and another area decorated in French Baroque lighted by a chandelier. Walls and columns were mirrored throughout the shoe department. Customers could also order handcrafted shoes to be made to order.

Above the shoe salon was the new men's shop. Kerr's had never had a separate men's shop before, and the new space allowed the store to design it from scratch. The shop covered two floors accessible by a suspended staircase. One part was modeled after a gentleman's club, with walls covered in green leather and rough wood, along with thick red and gray carpeting below. Along the walls were hung crests of notable medieval figures like Geoffrey Chaucer and the Duke of Kay. The upper level offered a fireplace and comfortable lounge chairs, as well as the latest newspapers and magazines.

Despite the postwar recession, Kerr's continued to do good business. Uptown in particular increased profits by 40 percent. In 1949, the store doubled its space by moving into the north half of the building, which had been occupied by a Safeway store.

With the passing of Ethel Toole Bulkley, W.S. Bulkley's widow, in 1952, a considerable amount of Kerr's stock became available. The following year, the board of directors sold a large interest in the store to Jerome M. Ney of Fort Smith, Arkansas, who would become Kerr's third president. Wyzanski retained his stock and moved up to chairman of the board. Wyzanski told a press conference that Ney would "add energetic and experienced direction."

Ney was, indeed, no rookie when it came to retail. His family's Boston Store had operated in Fort Smith and northwest Arkansas since 1879, and through his mother's (Maria Baer) family, he had a stake in the Stix, Baer and Fuller chain out of St. Louis (later acquired by Dillard's). When Ney took the reins, he expanded into Houston and Beaumont, Texas; Fayetteville,

Right: Entrance to the men's shoe salon, downtown. *Hillerman Collection; courtesy of the Oklahoma Historical Society.*

Below: By the 1940s, Kerr's had surpassed its major competitors in high-grade goods, especially in the realms of "better" menswear and luxurious surroundings. *Hillerman Collection; courtesy of the Oklahoma Historical Society.*

Arkansas; and later Denver. Kerr's was just part of his cobbled retail empire, and he maintained his residence in Fort Smith while vice-president Dulice O. Garrett (longtime Boston Store manager) shepherded the Kerr's stores and Ney's nephew, Leo Rodgers, oversaw most of the day-to-day operations.

Surveying the Oklahoma City landscape for high fashion competition, Ney found an opportunity in Balliet's. Edna Balliet had been a ready-to-wear manager at a store in Chickasha, and in 1936, she partnered with her husband, Fred, to open a boutique in Oklahoma City's exclusive Skirvin Hotel. Edna had an incredible acumen as a high fashion buyer and offered personalized service in dressing the city's elite. Just weeks after buying into Kerr's, Ney also bought Balliet's and offered the couple wide latitude to operate the store.

In 1955, yet another sweeping renovation took place at Kerr's, this time on the second floor. Presaging moves made by Dayton-Hudson at John A. Brown's a decade later, Garrett transformed the second floor into the "fashionable floor" and agglomerated all the trendiest merchandise there in addition to the shoe salon and beauty salon. With the shoe salon out of the way, $200,000 was spent expanding the men's shop into the entire floor and adding a suspended balcony above for the men's shoe department. Kerr's had always pampered the women shoppers, but this was the first time the men's shop offered a full line of men's merchandise.

Jerome N. Ney of Fort Smith, Arkansas, became Kerr's third president in 1953. He's pictured here outside the new Boston Store location in Fort Smith with his son, Randolph, in February 1972. *Courtesy of Randolph J. Ney.*

The Reding store at 4135 South Western Street opened in 1956. It was the last remaining location of the entire Kerr's Inc. stores by 1967. *Courtesy of the family of Edward Eason.*

Also in 1955, Milton Kamber contracted with Ney to install his Kamber's leather goods store on the mezzanine level. Kamber's family had operated a leather, luggage and gift store downtown since 1925. Kamber's, of course, became a legendary gift shop in Oklahoma City with its slogan, "You'll always find the unusual at Kamber's," and Milton's endearing wife, Eleanor, who appeared on live local television commercials for nearly fifty years.

At the same time downtown was under renovation, Ney and Garrett continued to be aggressive with their expansion plans. In cooperation with grocer and inventor-turned-developer Sylvan N. Goldman, Ney struck a deal to bring a Kerr's to Goldman's new Reding Shopping Center at Forty-Fourth and South Western Streets in 1956. Goldman courted Kerr's and Dodson's Cafeteria as the anchors for the center. The new Kerr's was a thirty-thousand-square-foot rectangular store of contemporary design in white brick and stone. As much an experiment as an expansion, the Reding demographic was not the same as, say, Uptown, and Garrett described the new store as a "miniature Kerr's" containing all the major departments as downtown but in a scaled-down version.

Soon after Reding opened, Ney entered into negotiations to secure Kerr's spot as an anchor at Penn Square alongside John A. Brown's and Montgomery Ward. According to Ney family sources, as plans moved

For unknown reasons, Kerr's was shut out of Penn Square in favor of longtime clothing retailer Rothschild's. In 1992, Rothschild's was acquired by Dillard's. *Photo by Joe Miller; Oklahoma Historical Society, the Gateway to Oklahoma History.*

forward, Ney ran into a heated disagreement with John Rooney of Manhattan Construction, the building contractor for the mall, and Kerr's was subsequently shut out of the development. It's not clear what the nature of the argument was, but it was sufficient to block one of Oklahoma City's oldest stores, and certainly its most prestigious, from the city's biggest regional shopping center. Though the ultimate demise of Kerr's was not directly related to being snubbed by Penn Square, observers still look at it as a turning point, the beginning of the end.

Shut out of Penn Square, Kerr's threw in with the developers of Capitol Gate, the proposed bigger and better development just west of Penn Square. In early 1957, developer R.F. Workman brought a plan before the city's planning commission seeking a zoning change for a regional shopping center known as Capitol Gate. A huge mixed-use development, its roughly seventy-five-acre site was larger even than downtown's commercial area. The area extended along May Avenue from Northwest Highway north to Northwest Sixty-Third Street and west of May Avenue to just east of Independence Avenue.

Capitol Gate drew immediate opposition from the Downtown Merchants Association and rival shopping center developers C.B. Warr and Ben

Wileman, all of whom appeared at commission hearings on the project's approval. The downtown association cited a Federal Reserve Bank report that said downtown had lost 32 percent of its trade to suburban shopping centers in recent years, and president George Sturm said downtown merchants were "barely holding their own." He also took a jab at city leaders for encouraging commercial sprawl because downtown merchants had to pay a higher tax rate than the suburban centers. Workman countered that the city shouldn't be favoring one district over another in the face of reasonable and fair competition. Besides, he had cash in hand from investors and a large department store already signed as the main anchor.

Capitol Gate was denied its zoning and was required to wait six months before reapplying. During the interim, an appeal to the city council failed. Unproven accusations swirled that some of the "nay" councilmen received large "campaign donations" by Wileman and others and that one "yea" voter lost quite a bit of business at his day job. The project was delayed further because the council wanted assurance that the project was properly financed. Workman, who had kept his angel investors and his anchor secret, was forced to reveal that his financier was already into the project for $20 million and that his anchor was Kerr's Department Store.

After nearly two years, the city council approved the site with a six-to-two vote. With bulldozers poised, Workman then learned his investors were in receivership and $13 million in the hole. The delays had proven too costly for the project. There are some indications the Kerr's store was to be an astounding 350,000 to 400,000 square feet, although it's likely nothing was solidified because the development ended up in quagmire and dissolution in 1960—the year Penn Square opened.

That year, 1960, was really the crucible for Kerr's Department Stores. True, there had been a steady expansion going back to 1936; however, the march to further suburbia was in full pace, and Kerr's was in danger of missing out. The lost opportunities of Penn Square and Capitol Gate were worrisome. The predicament was compounded by the fact that there were no new promising developments on the horizon that would allow Kerr's to compete with the likes of Brown's or Sears in the suburbs. What's more, one of the big three pillars—Halliburton's—fell in early 1961.

12

"The Miracle Centers"

In July 1961, customers and business leaders alike were shocked to learn from the national trade paper *Women's Wear Daily* that Jerome Ney and his associates had sold Kerr's to a syndicate of three brothers: Edward and Mitchell Eason and Irving Eisen. It remains a mystery why Ney sold out. He certainly didn't retire, as he continued to operate his other stores well into the 1970s. It was unlikely that financial necessity required the sale as all his stores, and Kerr's in particular, were doing well, although he may not have liked what he saw in the tea leaves for Kerr's future in Oklahoma City. Or perhaps the new ownership simply offered him more than he could refuse for the company.

Despite different last names, the three partners in the purchase were brothers. According to family tradition the brothers were born with name Eisen in Toronto, Ontario. There were nine children in the family raised by a single mother who eventually remarried and moved to the United States. The two younger brothers (and perhaps others) were left behind in Canada. After the boys suffered anti-Semitic bullying in school, their teacher changed their name to Eason. The boys later made their way to Melvindale, Michigan, outside Detroit.

By the 1950s, the Easons were owners of the Muzzy Brothers Department Store in Bristol, Connecticut. The brothers faced hardship within the retail trade, which makes the events of 1961 curiously compelling. Acknowledging debts of over $5 million, the Edward and Mitchell Eason accepted a bankruptcy order by federal courts in April. But on July 27, now partnered

Under Jerome Ney and continuing into the early Eason/Eisen leadership, Kerr's Downtown store remained a go-to destination for the finest goods, even as nationwide competitors were leaving Main Street. *Courtesy of the family of Edward Eason.*

Home Furnishings, Seventh Floor. *Courtesy of the family of Edward Eason.*

Women's Shoes Department, Second Floor. *Courtesy of the family of Edward Eason.*

with their elder brother, Irving, they purchased Kerr's for an undisclosed sum (estimated at $7.5 million). Then in October, a fire completely destroyed the Muzzy Brothers store in Bristol—a total loss. One month after the fire, Edward and Mitchell Eason and Ivan Eisen paid $5 million for the Blum's-Vogue haute couture boutiques in Chicago.

Structurally, Kerr's was incorporated as a Delaware corporation operating from New York, and Emil Horowitz and Hyman Friedman managed corporate finances from Manhattan. Eisen, president, moved to Chicago to oversee Blum's-Vogue and Edward Eason, vice-president, relocated to Oklahoma City to manage Kerr's. Henry Blum in Chicago was made chairman of the board.

The ownership group made rather dramatic and aggressive changes to the new Kerr's. The most surprising change ran seemingly counter to the other changes and to the image Kerr's had crafted in Oklahoma City for nearly sixty years. In September 1961, the Miracle Center concept was unveiled. The basement of the downtown store and about one-third of Reding's floor space were converted to discount merchandise, and a self-service system was installed. On entering the Miracle Center, customers grabbed a shopping cart or basket, selected their own merchandise and carried it to one of two checkouts—one for cash, one for credit. Miracle Center employees were dubbed "hosts" rather than salesclerks. Presumably, the Miracle Center was an attempt to compete with burgeoning discount stores like Spartan, Target and Kress, but it was a rather stark departure from Kerr's usual upscale offerings.

The new owners also aimed to expand the higher end of Kerr's base. After the Blum's-Vogue acquisition, the Mirror Room and "fashionable floor" were remodeled into a haute-couture salon. Essentially, the third floor became a Blum's-Vogue boutique within Kerr's and offered the same lines of merchandise as the Chicago stores. Edward Eason said, "It means the style-conscious woman of Oklahoma will have available to her the same selectivity and constant flow of new merchandise which residents of metropolitan Chicago now have. Blum's-Vogue at Kerr's will have guidance and assistance of the Chicago firm's buyers and specialists." Expansion was on the mind of Eisen in Chicago as well. The eight-story Blum's-Vogue

Under the Eason, Eisen and Horowitz leadership group, Kerr's Inc. maintained upscale offerings while acquiring retail stores throughout the upper Midwest. *Courtesy of the family of Edward Eason.*

The Miracle Centers at Reding and Shepherd Mall offered low-priced items, similar to TG&Y or Green's, that were not "markdowns" or clearance items. *Courtesy of the family of Edward Eason.*

building on the north side was to be replaced with a twenty-story "Cathedral of Fashion"; two floors were added to the Evanston, Illinois store; and two new suburban stores were added.

And Edward and Mitchell Eason and Irving Eisen didn't stop there. The following year, Kerr's Inc. paid $8 million for two large full-line department stores, the eighty-two-year-old Crosby Bros. store in Topeka, Kansas, and the one-hundred-year old Klaus in Chicago. In 1963, they created a Minnesota corporation and purchased the Emporium, the leading store in St. Paul, for an undisclosed price. Emil Horowitz became chairman of the board.

In the spring of 1963, Kerr's finally got the opportunity it had been desperately seeking since the Capitol Gate debacle—an anchor spot in a large suburban mall. In December 1960, developer Charles Jenkins won approval from the Oklahoma City Planning Commission to go forward with his Shepherd Plaza Shopping Center, which was to be constructed to the west of the big Sears, along Northwest Twenty-Third and following an L-shaped pattern northward along Villa Avenue. The prophecies of the adjacent neighborhood residents, whose protests had delayed the Sears development a decade earlier, were coming true. There were some protests to the city council, but nothing much came of them. The project went through as planned when the developers agreed to provide a park for the neighborhoods.

Renamed Shepherd Mall by the time it opened in September 1964, the mall was the city's first enclosed, air-conditioned shopping center and claimed to be the largest enclosed center west of the Mississippi, though at 742,000 square feet on fifty-four acres, it most likely did not hold that title for too long. Kerr's was tabbed as the anchor at the north end of the center in the spring of 1963, joining TG&Y on the east end and Penney's at the intersection of the two wings.

The new store, the fourteenth in the Kerr's Inc. national retail family, brought Kerr's even further from its established reputation as a high-end fashion apparel and home decorating store. The Shepherd Mall Kerr's

Even with the Miracle Centers in operation, Kerr's still offered one of the most well-stocked bargain basements in town. *Courtesy of the family of Edward Eason.*

At Shepherd Mall, Kerr's had the entire first floor, with the second floor used as a public banquet room. *Courtesy of the family of Edward Eason.*

The Kerr's wing of Shepherd Mall in 1965. *Photo by Tony Wood; Oklahoma Historical Society, the Gateway to Oklahoma History.*

offered a dizzying seventy-two departments, and dozens of full-page ads in the newspaper for the grand opening depicted things like home electronics, sporting goods and toys. Just two miles away, the longstanding Uptown store was folded into the Shepherd Mall store and closed soon after.

Despite the hope that the Shepherd Mall store offered to the long-term viability of Kerr's in Oklahoma City, it simply came too late to save the company. Several factors were coming to a head that, taken together, proved insurmountable. Externally, with urban renewal pending and the suburban exodus in full force, the downtown retail district was in retreat. Kerr's could hardly have been confident when early discussions about the optimistic "retail renaissance" specified a role for John A. Brown's and not it.

Locally, Kerr's Department Stores had moved too far from the policies and merchandise that had made them the fashion leader in Oklahoma City. Beginning with the Miracle Center and the reworking of Reding into something like an outlet store, shopping at Kerr's in the early 1960s had less of the cachet it once did.

The company was also expanding too much and too fast. Kerr's Inc. took on far too much debt in creating its fourteen-store chain. Beyond purchasing companies it could not afford, leadership made other questionable moves. For example, in 1964, amid the additional costs required for outfitting the Shepherd Mall store, Kerr's Inc. purchased the downtown store building from the heirs of original partner Frederick Lutz, from whom they had been leasing it. Purchasing property downtown in the urban renewal era was a risky endeavor, as one could not be assured that the property would not end up on the eminent domain list. The company explained that buying the building was part of the firm's overall expansion plans in Oklahoma. Plans were to add several million dollars' worth of new merchandise, including furniture, rugs, appliances and, inexplicably, a tire and auto supply store, to the Downtown store. The reason for the move became clear enough, however, when the building was promptly mortgaged for $750,000 within a day of the purchase.

Compounding the debt problem was that Eisen essentially gutted the equity of the companies after they were purchased by having them loan money to the corporate office to pay the debts accrued by the other stores. By February 1966, Kerr's Inc. had filed for Chapter XI bankruptcy, listing debts of over $6 million. Eisen told New York media, "Our downtown store has suffered badly from a deterioration of the downtown area in Oklahoma City and it is the main reason for our considerable operating loss." Claiming that 1965 losses at the hulking eight-story, 150,000-square-foot downtown store could not be made up by the successful Reding and Shepherd stores, Eisen opted to close the downtown store immediately in order to staunch the bleeding. When Edward Eason was contacted by local papers, he was taken completely by surprise, unaware of the actions taken in New York. On February 24, 1966, the downtown Kerr's closed for one week to reorganize.

Left: The signature downtown location closed its doors forever on March 18, 1966, a victim of too much expansion and changing shopping patterns. *Courtesy of the family of Edward Eason.*

Below: The "Neiman-Marcus of Oklahoma" went out quietly, with a public auction for stock and fixtures held the following week, June 28, 1967. *Photo by Jim Argo; Oklahoma Historical Society, The Gateway to Oklahoma History.*

Right: One of the final ads for Kerr's, 1967. *From the* Daily Oklahoman.

Below: The former Kerr's building sat vacant for eight years before succumbing to a wrecking ball on December 21, 1975. *Robert Allison Collection, RetroMetroOKC.*

It reopened with a court-ordered sale of the contents of the building, and on March 18, 1966, it closed permanently. There was no public eulogy for the old Kerr's as there would be for Brown's a few years later.

Even after the closing, Kerr's New York office was still not able to satisfy its creditors. In April, Shepherd Mall tried to evict Kerr's because its declining sales were adversely affecting the entire mall business. The eviction was delayed by the bankruptcy court in New York, but six months later, on September 3, the Shepherd Mall Kerr's store locked its doors for good. Reduced to just the Reding store and Balliet's in the Skirvin Hotel, Kerr's managed to stagger into 1967.

In March 1967, Balliet's was sold to an old familiar face. Kerr's former general manager Leo Rodgers, in partnership with Jerome Ney, purchased the boutique for a second time. Rodgers resided in Oklahoma City to operate the store, and Ney served as a hands-off chairman. Rodgers owned Balliet's for nearly twenty-five years before selling it in 1991.

The end of Kerr's came in the spring of 1967. And it was less than dignified. Gone were the sleek hand-drawn fashion models gracing the daily newspaper prints of old. The ads in these last days were full of exclamation points, with the letter *s* replaced by dollar signs and statements like "You'll be KERR-A Z Y to miss the savings!" and "We must raise cash!" Finally, on June 20, 1967, the Reding store closed for inventory and never reopened. Kerr's Department Store was dead just a few months shy of its sixtieth anniversary.

By the autumn of 1967, a TG&Y Family Center, somewhat fittingly, moved in to the Reding space. That autumn, Dillard's Brown-Dunkin made its first expansion into the Oklahoma City market by filling Kerr's vacant anchor spot in Shepherd Mall. Meanwhile, the downtown store became a dark, silent hulk for eight years. It fell to the urban renewal wrecking ball on December 21, 1975.

Part III

HALLIBURTON'S

13

"Oklahoma's Wonder Store"

Halliburton's Department Store was the first of the big three stores to fall, which is quite curious because, from a certain perspective, it was the most successful. And arguably its success led to its early end. Halliburton's origins are different from Brown's and Kerr's in that the store was not a colony from another state or an expansion of an existing store. It was founded earlier than the others during a distinctly different period in Oklahoma City history. Like the other two stores, however, Halliburton's was strongly influenced by its founder in both personality and circumstance.

Halliburton's grew to prominence from obscure beginnings on Oklahoma City's Main Street in 1898. So obscure were these beginnings that it's difficult to determine even what the name of the store was. In those days, the Main Street commercial district was confined to the stretch between Broadway and Robinson Streets while Grand (Sheridan) and California Avenues were equally busy. Main Street stores consisted of narrow twenty-five-foot-wide fronts extended back one hundred or so feet to an alley. Streets were muddy tracks rather than paved roads.

It was in one of these storefronts that Texas merchant Thomas Peabody Mellon opened a racket store at 138 West Main, on the south side of the street almost to the corner with Robinson. A racket store was much like the general store you see in western movies. They offered small quantities of a wide variety of merchandise and could be considered ancestors of the later five-and-dime stores. Competition was keen and plentiful in those days with Pettee's hardware store, the Lion Store and Max Herskowitz's Aurora Store, the most formidable of the bunch. Despite numerous sources mentioning the store, it's difficult to determine its name. Some sources refer to it as "Mellon's store," with "store" as a common noun and using "Mellon's" adjectivally rather than as a proper name. There's also evidence that the store might have been called the Fair. At any rate, by 1904 or so, the name Mellon's Dry Goods Company had gelled.

T.P. Mellon, called Peabody as boy, was born in 1869 on the steamboat landing in Beaumont, Texas. His father, Samuel, was the brother of noted Pittsburgh financier Andrew Mellon—an associate of Andrew Carnegie and later secretary of the treasury. Samuel operated a retail store in Beaumont but relocated to Lampasas, Texas, a few years later. Thus T.P. learned retailing firsthand from his father and, later, his mother, who took over the family store when Samuel died suddenly and mysteriously while visiting his brother in Pennsylvania the day before T.P.'s tenth birthday in 1879. At twenty-three, Mellon struck out on his own with $800 saved from his earnings at the family store. He ran a store in Temple, Texas, for several years before giving Oklahoma City a try in 1898.

Mellon had the day-to-day experience of running a small-town general store, but he lacked the formal training in the trade that helped forge the careers of Bert Brown and George Kerr. What Mellon did have was ambition and an intense drive that seemed to propel him into action. These traits were likely the result of his father's early death and his own battle with tuberculosis. Kerr and Brown took philosophical approaches to building their companies and securing their customer bases. But Mellon had a single, simple goal: to be the biggest store in the biggest city in the territory—and he achieved it in short order.

Of course, he had a foreshadowing of his future success on his first day in business. Working alone, it had taken him several days to prepare his store for opening and passersby had been peering in at his wares. On opening day, a large crowd gathered outside, which caused him some alarm. It happened that Sol Barth and Joe Myer had just arrived in the city and were looking for a location to open a menswear shop (they later owned B&M clothing store—as in Rothschild's B&M later—on Main Street for many years), so they leaned in and helped Mellon nearly sell out of goods that day. Mellon later claimed that on that day, he made a vow that within six years, he would have the largest department store in Oklahoma City.

In 1901, Oklahoma City was enjoying an economic boom. Having outgrown the store at 138 West Main and feeling that the city had outgrown it, too, Mellon purchased a building a few doors west and across Robinson

The Mellon's building at Main and Harvey Streets later became the Rothschild's Oklahoma City flagship store from 1927 until 1975. *RetroMetroOKC.*

at 204–06 West Main. The subsequent move doubled his floor space. For the first few years in the new location, the store was known as the Fair. By 1904, the name was simply Mellon's. Just as the new moniker was gaining recognition, a devastating fire gutted the building. Several firemen were injured, neighbors suffered from smoke inhalation and the contents of the store were a total loss.

Six months after the fire, Mellon had rebuilt the store, converting it from a simple dry goods store to a department store with upscale design and merchandise. Outside, a large sign made of white tile proclaimed in blue lettering the name "Mellon's," as did a tall metallic sign on the rooftop. The second floor, which had been apartments and a dentist's office, was finished out as a sales floor and a grand staircase diverged into two wings connected the floors. The windows and skylights were made of expensive prismatic glass, which provided plenty of natural light. Green silk curtains divided the fifteen departments, and plush seating encircled support columns. Newsmen called the new store "mammoth" and "the finest in the southwest." It seemed that one day short of six years after his arrival in Oklahoma City, Mellon owned the largest store in town. For his next work of fortune telling, Mellon predicted that he would one day have a six-story building on a Main Street corner lot.

T.P. Mellon continued to work determinedly to achieve his simple dream, which became increasingly difficult due to the ravages of tuberculosis. In October 1907, increased sales volume and the need for additional departments prompted Mellon to add a third floor to the store. However, around Thanksgiving that year Mellon suffered a severe tuberculosis attack that debilitated him for a month. On Christmas Day 1907, he felt well enough to go for a drive in the sunshine of a fifty-five-degree afternoon, but he suffered a relapse the next morning. He died on December 28 at the age of thirty-eight.

Mellon's obituary spoke admiringly of his indomitable will; he continued to work courageously in his last years even though his body was racked with pain. In a city where men who'd gone from rags to fabulous wealth could be found on every corner, the staggering fortune amassed by Thomas Peabody Mellon in just a few years was called phenomenal and "little short of marvelous."

Mary E. Mellon, whom T.P. had married in 1902, and Mary Ellen, her daughter from a previous marriage, were the sole heirs of the estate. In the event of a remarriage, the entirety of the estate would go to Mary Ellen. The store would continue, however. Just over a month after Mellon's death, Mrs. Mellon incorporated the Mellon Company, which included the store and the building. William Crane from Detroit became the principal shareholder in the company as well as its president, and Mrs. Mellon retained ownership of the building.

Mellon's continued to enjoy phenomenal growth, and in 1909, Crane secured a corner lot at Main and Harvey Streets and constructed a solid concrete and steel building with five stories and a basement. In succeeding years, despite continued growth, the company ran into a series of difficulties, including a dispute with a credit-clearing house in New York, which was detrimental to buying trips back East. The store also had a well-publicized disagreement with the *Daily Oklahoman* over ad rates. Both disputes involved lengthy and expensive lawsuits.

In 1914, Crane divested his shares in Mellon's, selling them to Milton Davenport Scott, who had been manager of the store since 1910. The company was reorganized with Scott as president, Russell Boyd Halliburton as secretary-treasurer and Leslie Eugene Abbott as superintendent. Regarding the takeover, Scott acknowledged that the store was already the biggest and most successful store in the city but added, "We hope to build the biggest concern in the southwest." The reorganized store was called Scott-Halliburton.

Russell Boyd Halliburton started at Mellon's and soon cultivated his own retail powerhouse. His stepdaughter later married future state senator Mike Monroney. *From* Oklahoma: A History of the State and Its People, *vol. 3, 1929.*

Russell Boyd Halliburton, a Missourian, had joined Mellon's in 1907 after five years' tutelage at Marshall Field in Chicago. Despite his title as secretary-treasurer, he was the guiding force behind Mellon's and Scott-Halliburton. It was largely Russell's business sense that continued the store on its upward trajectory. In 1916, the thirty-eight-year-old Halliburton strengthened his position in the company when he married Mellon's widow, Mary.

There were other family connections in the new business enterprise as well. Abbott was M.D. Scott's brother-in-law, having married Mae Scott when he and Abbott began their association back in Concordia, Kansas. In 1916, Abbott formed a partnership with Halliburton's brothers, Frederick Robert and James Cole Halliburton, to purchase (with M.D. Scott's investment) the Harlow Dry Goods Company in downtown Tulsa. The new store, Halliburton-Abbott, was an entirely independent operation and was not formally associated with Scott-Halliburton. It enjoyed moderate success until being purchased by Sears in 1947.

In November 1920, Scott-Halliburton fulfilled T.P. Mellon's final prediction by building a magnificent seven-story building on the northeast corner of Main and Hudson Streets (a mezzanine level made it technically eight floors). The store already had a reputation for offering top-shelf merchandise—and lots of it—but the huge new building with its sleek and modern design only cemented its position. Most notable about the move was its address. In 1920, the corner of Main and Hudson Streets, though only three blocks from Broadway, was considered quite far from the epicenter of the commercial life of Oklahoma City. Scott-Halliburton's move essentially shifted the retail axis of downtown. To an outsider, especially an East Coast investor, Scott-Halliburton was the only store in Oklahoma City that could compare to the great retail houses in America's large cities. Brown's and Kerr's were still years away from approaching anything like Scott-Halliburton, and no other store in the city could offer so much merchandise under one roof.

Halliburton's was arguably the best-equipped department in the state in its early days. Even local hero and film star Tom Mix stopped in during a 1929 visit. *Frank Stuart collection; courtesy of the Oklahoma Historical Society.*

A year after the new store opened, a group of investors headed by Samuel Moses Gloyd and Wade Hampton purchased M.D. Scott's interest in the company. Asked about the sale publicly, Scott simply said the price they offered him was too good to turn down. A week later, he opened the M.D. Scott Dry Goods Company at 307–09 West Main. He was bankrupt just over a year later and returned to Kansas, where he died the same day as Bert Brown in 1940.

At age fifty-six, Samuel Gloyd was already an established businessman when he purchased controlling interest in the store. A Missourian like Halliburton, Gloyd established a successful retail lumber operation in Kansas and then expanded into Oklahoma City in 1897. He established a diversified portfolio of building material companies and real estate holdings all across the Southwest. The new endeavor was renamed Gloyd-Halliburton, and he served as board chairman while Halliburton continued in his role at the store's helm.

Ultimately, the store was a departure from the investments Gloyd usually made. Only three years later, in January 1925, he and Hampton sold out their interests to Harold Daniel McEwen from Wichita, Kansas. Details on the deal were not disclosed, but observers put the transaction at about $1 million. Gloyd cautioned people about reading anything into his exit from the company. He simply wasn't comfortable in retail, and as he was one of the wealthiest men in Oklahoma City, the store was only a small portion of his business interests. The buyout meant nothing except a willingness on his part to be relieved of an enterprise that demanded so much of his personal attention. As per tradition, the store's name was changed—to McEwen-Halliburton. Under Russell's watchful leadership, the transition was smooth.

That's not to say that everything remained the same. McEwen was not the hands-off silent partner that Halliburton was used to having in the seventh-floor offices. At just thirty-two years of age, McEwen was an energetic entrepreneur. A college graduate and veteran of the world war, he had worked in his family's wholesale grocery business in Wichita and also built and ran a hotel there. Despite his apparent work ethic, it's not entirely clear where he was able to obtain the $1 million to buy out Gloyd at such a young age. Perhaps the answer lay in his marriage, in 1921, to Evelyn Rorabaugh, A.O. Rorabaugh's daughter and Bert Brown's cousin.

As it happened, McEwen was not destined to work with Russell for too long. In July 1927, Halliburton traveled to Europe on a buying trip for the store but became ill while overseas. He returned home only to discover he'd been stricken with influenza. Three agony-filled months later, Russell Boyd Halliburton, age forty-eight, died from the aftereffects of the virus on September 3, 1927. Curiously, the deaths of the three major figures most associated with each of the big three stores arose from complications during buying trips.

Despite his perpetual second billing, it was Russell Halliburton who took T.P. Mellon's dream and crafted the store from a large dry goods store into what was then Oklahoma City's largest and finest department store. As funeral preparations were made, the store's advertising editor became Halliburton's eulogist:

> *Those who worked with him for years and know the beauty and consolation of his courteous sympathy are not thinking today of a loyal employer called away from life; they are thinking of a genuine friend who was unfailing in his kindness and always met them with respect.*

> *The success that Russell Boyd Halliburton achieved in business circles was no mean success. He succeeded well in developing a splendid business. He stood among the men who have made Oklahoma City the metropolis of a great young state.*
>
> *But greater still was the success that crowned him among associates and subordinates. His greatest success was builded* [sic] *in the hearts of those made happy by his genial life, and desolate by the tidings of his untimely death. The tears that fall upon his grave today bear proof that his was a splendid soul.*

In the succeeding years after Halliburton's death, McEwen ran the store without a managing partner, though presumably Halliburton's shares were held by his widow or brothers. Despite no outward signs of a decline in store quality or any financial difficulty, McEwen-Halliburton ran into the shoals. In May 1932, the store filed for reorganization in the court. J. Cole Halliburton was installed as company president and managed the repayment of the majority of company debt. Harold McEwen was reduced to a secondary role but did not lose his shares, and the name of the store did not change. In January 1933, the courts placed the company into receivership despite J. Cole Halliburton's assertions that the store's assets easily eclipsed its much-reduced debt. Jeweler and former Oklahoma City mayor Walter C. Dean was named receiver though McEwen and J. Cole Halliburton were retained as vice-presidents.

14

"The Store with the Friendly Spirit"

After nearly five years in receivership, Halliburton's announced on November 11, 1937, that all stock in the company had been purchased by Erle Palmer Halliburton. A distant cousin of J. Cole and Russell, Erle Halliburton was already fabulously wealthy when he bought the store. Using skills he learned in the U.S. Navy and in the oil fields of California, Halliburton devised a method of using cement to contain and control oil wells. Purchasing a store was not an anomaly for him since by 1937, he had a reputation for diversifying his holdings rather widely—he founded the short-lived yet influential S.A.F.E.Way Airlines (with J. Cole Halliburton as controller) in Tulsa—and held numerous other companies unrelated to oil production. With Harold McEwen out of the picture, J. Cole Halliburton became the general manager and the store name was changed to simply Halliburton's, though it now referred exclusively to his cousin, Erle P. Halliburton.

Announcing the change, the company produced the following newspaper ad:

> *GOOD MORNING! A name already known, yes famous, to all Oklahomans and the entire Southwest greets you! Halliburton's. For 39 years, dating back to 1898, this store has recognized the supremacy of finest quality and value for it's* [sic] *customers. It has thought earnestly, incessantly, and intelligently of your needs and wants and supplying those necessities with the best that America produces. It has always been the kind*

we could tell facts about. Halliburton's was the first to pioneer the "west on Main Street" movement, dating back to 1920, now recognized as the heart of the shopping center of Oklahoma City. Now—this friendly old store is carrying on...rising to still greater heights to serve more satisfactorily and completely the fine people of our city, state, and the Southwest.

Almost immediately, the store underwent an expansion and modernization program. A few weeks after Erle Halliburton took ownership, the company purchased the entirety of the building on Main and Hudson Streets from its partial owners. An eighth floor was added to the building soon after, and the entire building was cooled by central air conditioning by the summer of 1938—fully a decade before Kerr's and Brown's attempted air conditioning.

Flush with Erle Halliburton's cash and equipped with a large, modern building, Halliburton's flourished for the next decade under the able leadership of J. Cole Halliburton. By late 1947, the store was still the largest and most notable store in Oklahoma City. John A. Brown's and Kerr's were certainly gaining on it in terms of size (Brown's) and quality (Kerr's), and they had something more that Halliburton's didn't—the love of the people. As noted, Brown's carefully cultivated its role as "the people's store." As for Kerr's, it was not as loved as Brown's, but it had taken the successful route of creating a marvelous shopping experience, bringing the best of the world to Oklahoma City. Halliburton's, the former frontrunner, appeared interested only in being the biggest and the best, without securing the favor of Oklahoma Cityans.

Outside the city, however, Halliburton's was a pearl for acquisitive retailers. In October 1947, Federated Department Stores came calling. Federated was a conglomerate of six retailing companies of the finest pedigree—Bloomingdale's of New York, Abraham & Straus of Brooklyn, Filene's of Boston and Lazarus and Shillito's of Ohio. Its postwar expansion plan was centered on purchasing the biggest and best stores in the Southwest, anticipating a Sunbelt boom. In anticipation, Federated also purchased Foley's in Houston and Sanger Brothers in Dallas. As usual, terms were not discussed, but J. Cole Halliburton said the price was "several millions."

John H. O'Toole arrived from Brooklyn to head the store, which remained under the Halliburton's name. Customers were receptive to seeing the same goods they could find in the big stores back East, and in 1949, company officials reported that Halliburton's had shattered its own sales records. But in 1951, Federated made a change in company policy that ultimately spelled doom for Halliburton's.

In 1938, Halliburton's became the first of the big three retailers to install air conditioning. *Photo from 1945, Hillerman collection; courtesy of the Oklahoma Historical Society.*

A new division called Fedway was created in 1951 to further refine the parent company's interest in the Southwest and its concern over the rapid suburbanization happening nationally—and what that meant for downtown retail. Whereas Federated had always purchased existing stores with strong

This ad from January 16, 1961, provides no indication that Halliburton's would close for good in less than a week. *From the* Daily Oklahoman.

reputations, Fedway would identify dynamic, booming cities and build entirely new stores there. Fedway believed there was still a place for retail in the central business district, and its stores were to be new and modern, which meant a necessary inclusion for ample parking. Wichita Falls, Corpus Christi and Amarillo, Texas, as well as Albuquerque, New Mexico, were among the first Fedway stores to be built.

In effect, this policy left Halliburton's bereft at the corporate table, as it was much smaller than its eastern siblings. Also, the economic conditions in

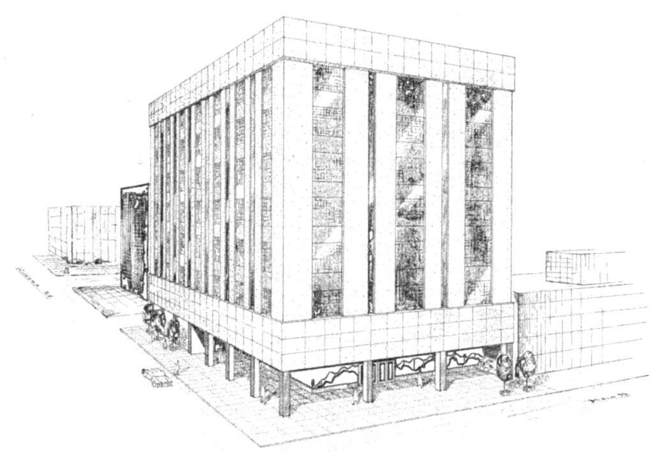

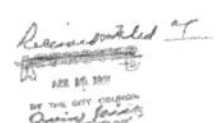

Original plans for the Center Building included an exterior remake and a completely renovated interior. *Courtesy of the City of Oklahoma City, City Clerk's Office Archives.*

The demolition of the Halliburton Building on April 17, 1977, effectively closed the chapter on the heyday of Oklahoma City's downtown shopping days. Photo Monty Reed. *Oklahoma Historical Society, the Gateway to Oklahoma History.*

downtown Oklahoma City—most notably a lack of parking and widespread absentee ownership—made it virtually impossible for Halliburton's to become a full member of the Fedway family. Moving through the 1950s, the suburbanization trend and the general decline of downtown Oklahoma City forced Fedway to reevaluate Halliburton's position. By the end of the decade, company leaders believed they faced two alternatives: they could join the suburban train and invest in new stores or reach profitability by cutting back operations below company standards.

They chose a third alternative. At 5:00 p.m. on Saturday, January 21, 1961, store manager R.M. Barksdale locked the doors to Halliburton's for the last time. The news came as a shock to city shoppers and businessmen, as there had been no indication such a move could happen. After a sixty-two-year run—most of it spent at the top of the retail heap—the first of the big three stores had fallen.

In 1964, the long-vacant Halliburton building was acquired by the City of Oklahoma City for $205,000 and renovated into municipal office space. Renamed the Center Building, it served as city offices until 1974, when it was sold to the Urban Renewal Authority for planned Galleria space.

Epilogue
"Respectfully..."

I remember John A. Brown had two delivery runs a day. My mother would call in the morning, and the merchandise would be delivered that afternoon. The clerks in the downtown store used No. 2 pencils for writing up sales and had a system of overhead pneumatic tubes they used for payment. We used to go to Kerr's and Halliburton's, but Brown's was the one my mother favored.

—Jim N.

My aunt, Mrs. Alice Wallace, was the John A. Brown's purchasing agent for women's foundations and lingerie for almost fifty years. Her job took her all over the world. In the '50s, when I was just a child, she would fascinate me with stories of her travels and adventures in the Orient, Occupied China, Japan and Europe. Aunt Alice would show me keepsakes given to her by dignitaries in these places, as she was considered as some kind of royalty from the United States—quite an accomplishment for a farm girl from Crescent, Oklahoma.

—Rocky M.

My father was pastor of Downtown Baptist Church [at] *629 West Main for thirty-five years, starting in 1935, so I grew up visiting all those great stores. My mother would put on her hose, hat and gloves and we would spend the day shopping—with rest stops on Kerr's balcony rest area and*

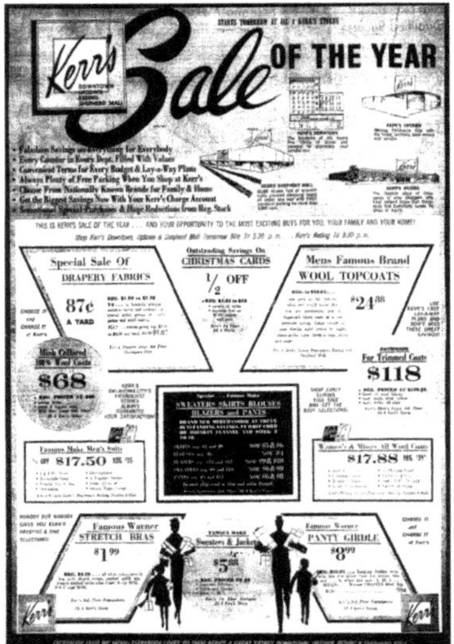

Kerr's ad showing all four locations, 1965. *From the* Daily Oklahoman.

lunch at Anna Maude's and ending with the dime stores where she always bought orange slices to take home

—Laverne M.

I worked at both Kerr's and John A. Brown in advertising. At Kerr's, we based the women's faces on Lana Turner. I even met my husband at Kerr's. His navy reserve unit was called up for Korea, and when we returned, Kerr's was either gone or almost gone. I did freelance artwork after that for Peyton-Marcus, Street's and Brown's. When Dayton-Hudson bought the store, I lost my freelance account because I was "too old." I couldn't have even been forty.

—Frances E.

As a child from a town of 1,200 people, to me, Brown's seemed huge. I was careful to stay within sight of Mother because of all of the floors and passageways. I couldn't seem to get fixed in my mind which direction we were going and what department connected to what other department. I was a child who had no qualms about wandering through the canyons several miles from my home and never getting lost.

One day, I saw that there were some African American adolescents and children sitting and standing near the luncheonette at Brown's but didn't know what was going on. On this day in August 1958, I noticed these people because they were black but paid little attention and went on about my business. Later, Clara Luper became one of my main heroes as I studied and taught multicultural studies and realized what was happening there. I believe Clara Luper wasn't given enough credit nationally for what she and these young people started. Other sit-ins are more famous, but the downtown Oklahoma City one predates them. And Mrs. Luper said that Mrs. Brown and she became good friends when they finally got together and the decision was made to integrate all the facilities of the store.

—Karen Mc.

My mother worked at J.A.B. downtown during World War II. She married my dad before war's end and moved to Wewoka. I began working at John A. Brown's in 1974 at Crossroads Mall by doing inventory before the store opened. In 1977, I went to auditing, which was located in the old Capitol Hill store. I stayed there until January 1979. I will tell you that my husband did not move to Oklahoma City until 1972 so only saw Brown's as it was at Crossroads and grew tired of hearing from people about how great Brown's was…like it was Disneyland or something!

—Susan C.

I worked downtown from December 1951 to April 1984, so I did enjoy the three department stores. But Brown's was always my favorite because it had everything. *Many a lunch hour I spent just browsing through the different departments. My office was only a block away, so I could be there in a flash. I think of Brown's as having been a small version of Harrods in London. On a hot day like today, I am reminded, that it was one of the last commercial businesses to put in air-conditioning.*

—Tula F.

I grew up about four blocks from Capitol Hill. It was a great day in the late 1940s and early 1950s when I went shopping downtown with my mom. She was always dressed well—as though we were going to church. Dressing well included a hat. My dad always dropped us off at the "back door" of John A. Brown's on Park Avenue. There was a seating area there for that purpose. The area was outside but was sheltered from the elements. That door was just outside the china department.

—Judy B.

Brown's was a "one stop shop," 1968. *From the* Daily Oklahoman.

I'm fifty-nine and have lived in Oklahoma City all my life. I remember shopping downtown with my mother when I was young—so late '50s/ early '60s. Mother always dressed up to go shopping like it was a special occasion: nice dress, jewelry, high heels and white gloves. My fondest memory is that of a large stuffed lion in the men's department. I think it was a real lion (I certainly thought it was then!), but now I suppose it could've been a stuffed toy. It was big (to a little girl) and sat atop a glass shelf over one of the clothing racks. If a little girl were to ask politely, the clerk would press a hidden button, and the lion would roar! I've often wondered what happened to that lion.

—S.W.

I came on the bus from a much smaller town and thought I had arrived in New York City in the late 1950s. I lived at the YWCA on Park and worked at Kerr's Department Store in the beauty salon until 1960. The first-floor front entrance was beautiful with marble floors. Perfume, makeup, jewelry and accessories I remember the most.

—Kay F.

Halliburton's had the best prices back then. I personally didn't like to shop at Kerr's because I thought their salespeople were kind of snotty, and since I was just a simple working young girl, I really could not afford their prices.

—Suzanne P.

Halliurton's, 1941. *From the* Daily Oklahoman.

I am pleased to say that I started my fashion-merchandising career at Kerr's in 1941, working part time

Showing off, Kerr's style, 1947. *From the* Daily Oklahoman.

and vacations while in high school, and continued from 1943 to 1947 during my years at Oklahoma University. My mentor during those years was Ruth Meyers (Butler at that time). After graduation, I continued working for Kerr's as an assistant buyer, manager of their Norman store and then a buyer at downtown. In 1952, I went to Halliburton's as their sportswear buyer until 1954, when I moved to Denver.

Mr. and Mrs. Wyzanski urged me to go to Halliburton's when they knew they were selling the store. I left Kerr's and got the Halliburton's job the same day. I believe they moved to Portugal later on.

—Donna D.

On June 2, 1972, I walked down the isle on the arm of my eighty-eighty-year-old white-haired grandfather, who proudly stepped in for my dad to give me away. It was a bittersweet day but one of great joy, and John A. Brown's was a big part of it. My sweetheart and I celebrated forty-one years this past June. I'm hoping maybe a granddaughter will someday want a vintage dress for her special day.

—Susan R.

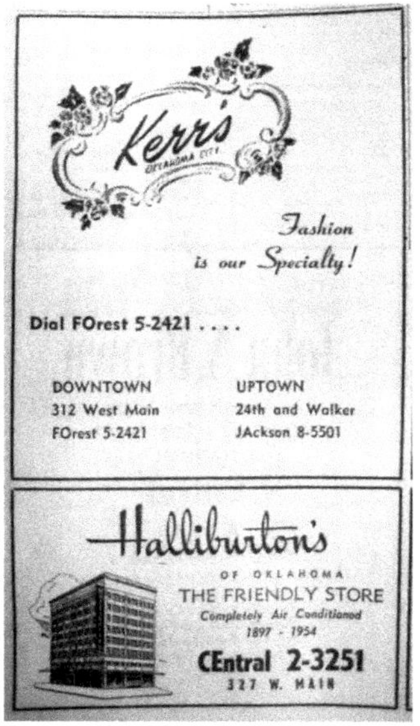

Kerr's as Halliburton's Yellow Pages ads, 1954. *Oklahoma City Telephone Directory.*

I worked at John A. Brown's from 1981 to 1982, when I was a senior in high school. Loved that job. Our undercover security guard caught two ladies stealing clothes in the dressing room in juniors. Chased them through the store with the security for Royal Doulton rep following behind. Shoplifter ran into traffic on Pennsylvania and our security lady had on cowboy boots. She did finally catch her, but she thought she was going to have a heart attack afterward. The shoplifter had convinced some patron in the parking lot that our security was trying to attack her and let the shoplifter into her car and then it began a car chase. When the patron figured out [what] *was really going on, she made the shoplifter get out of the car. That was a helluva a day!*

—Kim W.

In the early 1970s, I was hired by John A. Brown's as a sales clerk. I remember being enthralled by the money chutes that went throughout the store. I also remember my feet hurt so badly that I could hardly stand. I went to the ladies' room, where an attendant told me to put my feet in the toilet and flush for relief of the pain. It worked!

—Sharon L.

The Brown's employees' cafeteria was on the top floor. It had a counter and tables inside. A wall of windows overlooked the roof terrace. Employees could take their food and eat on the tables out there. People went out there to smoke also. It was decorated with trees and flowers in pots. The terrace adjoined two buildings. All of it looked old—like it had been there awhile.

—Janet K.

When I worked at Kerr's Uptown, I knew that suburban shopping was the future! The volume of Uptown and the lower—much lower—overhead compared to Downtown was big. Profit wise, that Uptown store made more money. But Downtown was nicer. There were these chandeliers in Wizzy's (Mrs. Wyzanski) office that the new owners took out, and the store became junky. I think the chandeliers are in the Getty Museum in Los Angeles.

—*Clara R.*

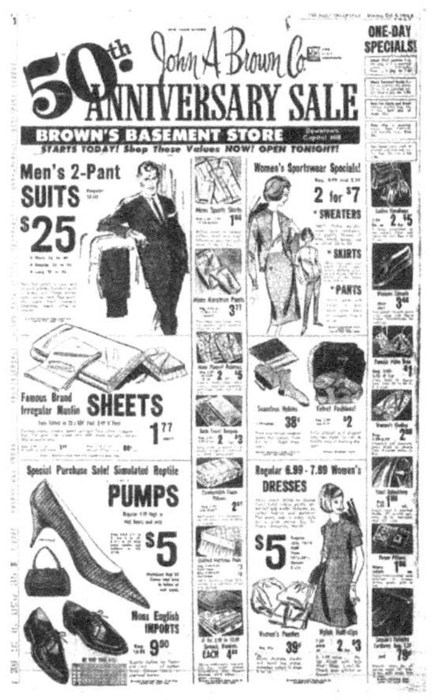

John A. Brown, 1965. *From the* Daily Oklahoman.

I was a stock boy from Brown's downtown. Many of the clerks were older women, but I heard Della told staff, "As long as you can get here, you can work for me." The floor walkers were in charge of catching shoplifters, and that often involved running in circles around the sale tables.

—*Dale F.*

In 1952, I got a job at Kerr's and traveled from El Reno by interurban. In one summer, I furnished my house from Kerr's, so all I earned went right back to Kerr's!

—*Virginia M.*

Dillard's wanted that Penn Square store more than anything! When I worked at the makeup counter there, we made more profit than any other department store in the Southwest.

—*Cheryl R.*

My mother bought some Haviland china from Rorabaugh-Brown and hid it under the bed so my father wouldn't find out. Later, I would go into Brown's with my mother. We had a run-in with a clerk in millinery, but my mother excused her as "being tired." She told me, "When your feet hurt you hurt all over."

Ad for Kerr's Uptown, 1937. *From the* Daily Oklahoman.

Another time, I borrowed my dad's car and went shopping downtown. I parked in the lot behind Kerr's, left the car and realized I didn't have any cash! I had to track down an old beau that worked downtown and get money to get the car out!"

—*Mary B.*

I planned to work at Brown's for five years, but loved it so much I stayed for ten! When I heard they were demolishing the downtown store, I went down and took several of the sidewalk tiles.

—*Renata T.*

In 1964, I had [just] *moved back from California. I could not find bikinis anywhere! I went to Kerr's and bought bikinis for my first club, Lil' Abner's. The request shocked the sales clerk, and she suggested something "less skimpy." I opened up the first go-go bar in Oklahoma City on Eighth and Walker. They probably have no idea of how much I made off of those bikinis!*

—*Jan B.*

My mother preferred to shop in Capitol Hill since you didn't have to get dressed up in hats and gloves like downtown. I bought my wedding dress at Kerr's but not the veil. Finally, my soon-to-be husband and I went look at veils. He sat in the car while I made up my mind. By the time I left the store, he was so mad that we almost didn't get married!

—*Linda B.*

All of those stores were neat. But at Kerr's, I used to throw my mother's coat from the mezzanine to the first floor! She wasn't happy about it, but I thought it was fun.

—*Joe B.*

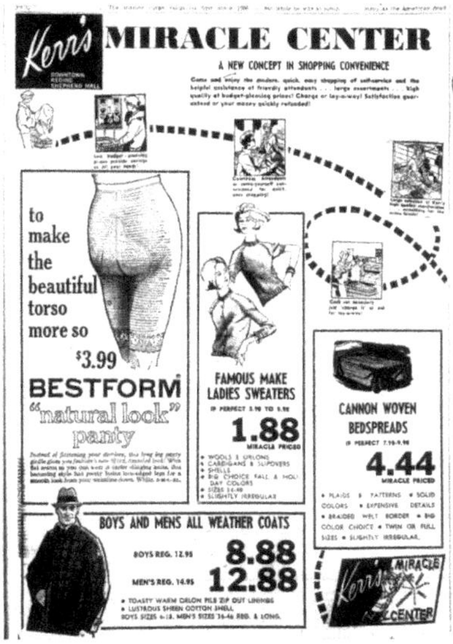

Kerr's Miracle Centers, 1965. *From the* Daily Oklahoman.

I was hired as an assistant buyer for Brown's in 1976. I worked at the converted Capitol Hill location. The offices were cubicles that did not go all the way to the ceiling, so when an assistant buyer got reamed out over a mistake, the WHOLE building knew about it! [One story] *I'd heard was that Mrs. Brown was so frugal that for a new pencil, you had to turn in the old pencil stub to her. And, yes, I heard that story from more than one person!*

—Pam F.

Bibliography

Ambrose, Laura to Eliot Lyon, n.d.

Brown, Charles. Interview by Ajax Delvecki. Oklahoma City, June 27, 2013.

Daily Oklahoman.

Douglas, Donna. Interview by Ajax Delvecki. Oklahoma City, July 17, 2013.

Hill, L.B. *A History of the State of Oklahoma*. Chicago: Lewis Publishing Company, 1908.

Kerr, W.F., and Ina Gainer. *The Story of Oklahoma City, Oklahoma: "The Biggest Little City in the World."* Chicago: S.J. Clarke, 1922.

Lemmons, Molly, and Bambi Dunn. *Oklahoma Voices: Molly Lemmons*. Oklahoma City, OK: Metropolitan Library System, 2007.

Lewelling, Madeline. "Eliot Grosvenor Lyon." Unpublished notes, 1972.

Life on the Line: The Dodson's Cafeteria Story. Oklahoma City, OK: Forty-Sixth Star Press, 2010.

Luper, Clara. *Behold the Walls*. [Oklahoma City?]: Jim Wire, 1979.

Ney, Randolph J. Interview by Ajax Delvecki. Oklahoma City, July 4, 2013.

Oklahoma City Times, 1908.

Oklahoma Journal, 1964.

Rosenberg, Leon Joseph. *Dillard's: The First Fifty Years*. Fayetteville: University of Arkansas Press, 1988.

The Sooner: Yearbook of the University of Oklahoma. Norman: University of Oklahoma, 1941.

Thoburn, Joseph B., and Muriel H. Wright. *Oklahoma: A History of the State and Its People*. New York: Lewis Historical Publishing Company, 1929.

Tulsa Daily World, 1927.

Additional Resources

City of Oklahoma City. http://www.okc.gov.

Metropolitan Library System. *Oklahoma Images.* http://cybermarsx.mls.lib.ok.us/okimages/okimages.asp.

Oklahoma Historical Research Center. http://www.okhistory.org/research/index?full.

Oklahoma Historical Society. *Gateway to Oklahoma History*. http://gateway.okhistory.org.

RetroMetroOKC. http://www.retrometrookc.org.

Index

A

Abbott, Leslie Eugene 132
Ambrose, Laura 31, 45, 46, 60, 76, 80
Arbee, Marilyn 37, 48

B

Balliet's 112, 126
Brown, Della Mae Dunkin 64
  character 46, 59
  reclusiveness 44
  youth 43
Brown Dry Goods Company 28
Brown-Dunkin Company 23, 60
Brown, John A.
  character 26, 29, 35, 38
  death 41
  youth 27
Bulkley, Charles Gideon 100
Bulkley, Willard Spencer 100, 104, 108

C

Capitol Gate Shopping Center 114
Classen, Anton 11

D

Dayton-Hudson Corporation 78
  Target stores 94
Dillard's Inc. 78
  history 25
Dillard, William Thomas 23
Dunkin, John H. 36, 38, 60

E

Eason, Edward 116, 118, 123
Eason, Mitchell 116
Eaton's Department Store 97
Eisen, Irving 116, 118, 123

F

Federated Department Stores 138, 139
Friendagon 83

G

Gloyd-Halliburton store 134
Gloyd, Samuel Moses 134

H

Halliburton-Abbott store 133
Halliburton, Erle Palmer 137
Halliburton, James Cole 133, 136, 137, 138
Halliburton, Russell Boyd 132, 135
Halliburton's 129, 138

J

John A. Brown Company
- Brown's Annex 50
- Brown's College Corner 48
- buildings 37
- Capitol Hill store 87
- Downtown store 31, 37, 51, 54, 81, 83, 85
- policies 30, 32, 35, 40, 46, 61
- sale to Dayton-Hudson Corporation 78
- sale to Dillard's Inc. 22, 25
- warehouse 48

K

Kamber's 113
Katz Drug Store 49, 60
Kennedy Brothers Dry Goods Company 99
Kerr, George Gabriel 100, 101
Kerr's 100
- Downtown store 101, 104, 112, 126
- Miracle Centers 118
- Mirror Room 109, 119
- Norman store 105
- policies 100, 101, 104, 109
- Reding store 113, 123, 126
- Shepherd Mall store 121, 123, 126
- Uptown store 105, 107, 122

L

Luper, Clara 66, 75
Lutz, Frederick O. 100, 101, 123
Lyon, Eliot 26, 31

M

Mandel Brothers store 99, 108
McEwen-Halliburton store 135
McEwen, Harold Daniel 135, 136
Mellon's store 130, 131
Mellon, Thomas Peabody 129, 130, 132

N

Ney, Jerome M. 110, 116
Nichols Hills 42, 43

O

Oklahoma City
- business district 11
- land run 10

Main Street shopping district 51, 56, 71, 73, 129, 133
rivalry with Guthrie 11
Overholser, Henry 10

P

Penn Square Mall 59, 67, 70, 113
Pettee, William J. 9

Q

Quail Springs Mall 88

R

Rodgers, Leo 112
Rorabaugh, Anson Otterbean 27
Rorabaugh-Brown Dry Goods Company 29

S

Scott-Halliburton store 132
Scott, Milton Davenport 103, 132, 134
Shepherd Mall 120
Sherburne, James 80, 84, 89
S&H Green Stamps 76
sit-ins 66
suburbanization 13, 17, 59, 139

U

urban renewal 15, 72, 83, 87
Urschel, Charles
kidnapping 44

W

Wade, Frank 62
Wileman, Ben 58, 67
Wyzanski, Henry N. 108, 110

Ajax Delvecki (left) and Larry Johnson (right) at the former Brown's Campus Corner location, 2016. *Photo by Jay Hughes.*

About the Authors

Ajax Delvecki is a third-generation Oklahoma City resident with a longtime interest in past city retail, especially stores he can remember like John A. Brown's, Emmer Brothers and TG&Y. He enjoys collecting old department store memorabilia and researching downtown retail history—any city or town will do. He can be reached at okcstores@yahoo.com

Larry Johnson is a bookish historian who finds himself most at home in the broad sweeping plains of northwestern Oklahoma, even though his travels have extended beyond the Atlantic. He has a noisy dog, an even noisier daughter and a wife to rival his love of books. His first job for wages was at the John A. Brown Penn Square store in 1981.